The Little Village That Could

The Untold Story of Devereux Heights

by

Kenneth C. Mitchell

Seagull Press
Springfield, Illinois
2019

2nd Printing, September 2019
Printed in the U.S.A. by Capitol Blue Print, Springfield, IL
Cover design by Tony Sanguedolce

Published by:
Seagull Press
2 Oakwood Road
Springfield, IL 62711
(217) 787-7100

What Others Are Saying about This Book

Our community is built on the passion, dedication and hard work of our residents. I appreciate Ken's devotion in communicating these stories about Springfield and allowing the history of our city be shared through others' knowledge and experiences. —**Jim Langfelder**, *Life-long resident and Springfield Mayor*

Ken Mitchell's fascination with the village of Devereux Heights is contagious and the first-hand interviews make the village and the period a personal experience. The village is not that far away and the time not that long ago, but I was intrigued by the lifestyle of these coal mining families and how much has changed in just a generation or two. —**Mark McDonald**, Producer/ Host, "Illinois Stories", WSEC PBS

Every neighborhood and town needs an industrious historian like Ken Mitchell. In his latest book, he transforms Devereux Heights from an obscure name on a map into a real place. –**James Krohe Jr.**, journalist, local historian, and author. His latest book is *Corn Kings & One-Horse Thieves: A Plain-Spoken History of Mid-Illinois.*

True to form, author Kenneth Mitchell has once again captured the heart and soul of what might have otherwise been a forgotten community and its people who helped shape today's Springfield and Sangamon County. Devereux's history was a story waiting to be told and Mitchell has done it beautifully and thoroughly. —**Vicky Whitaker**, President of the Sangamon County Historical Society.

This book is a wonderful history of a little part of Springfield. I wish we had more books like it for different parts of the city that have their own unique story. –**Curtis Mann**, Director of the Sangamon Valley Collection of the Lincoln Library and local history author.

Ken Mitchell has earned the richly deserved reputation as the raconteur of the North End of Springfield. He has brought to life the many interesting stories of the neighborhood—and his latest book, The Little Village That Could: The Untold Story of Devereux Heights—*is no exception. Through his talent for meticulous research and documentation, Mitchell gives the village on Springfield's north side its due. Readers will discover delightful insights into the culture and histories of the largely ethnic families that settled in the village originally tied, like many other small Illinois communities, to coal mining.*–**Taylor Pensoneau**, Illinois Author and Historian.

I had a difficult time putting the book down because I wanted to keep reading it way past my normal bedtime. It seems all the old stories told to me by my father and grandfather came rushing back to me and it was a very emotional read for me. Loved it much.—**Dominic Giacomini,** who grew up in Devereux Heights

After many years in Springfield, I thought I knew the city, but I didn't know the story of Devereux Heights. Ken Mitchell shines a spotlight on this hidden north-end village and brings its history to life. His research and interviews with older Devereux residents reveal a tight-knit immigrant community whose men labored in coal mines, as they and their families struggled to learn the language and ways of a new country while honoring old-world traditions. The Little Village That Could is a heartwarming read. –**Virginia Scott**, Former Director, Illinois Environmental Council and community volunteer

A very enjoyable and interesting read. My closest friend growing up lived on Donna Street. We spent a lot of days and nights exploring many of the locations mentioned in this book. Thank you for resurrecting numerous memories. **Joe Giacomini**, whose family settled in Devereux Heights.

This really brings Devereux to life. Really enjoyed reading it. –**Jim and Nancy Bartlett**, residents of Devereux Heights.

This book is very informative, as well as educational. It tells a story of a part of town that is often overlooked. It tells of the struggles of the immigrants who came from the old countries to settle over here and of the only work that they could find. Finally, it tells of the daily struggles that they endured and their gains and setbacks, so that their children and their grandchildren would have a better life.—**Bob and Mary Yoggerst**, residents of Devereux Heights.

Author Ken Mitchell has really out done himself publishing the realistic history of the Deveraux Heights Neighborhood. What an exciting account of the past, and I'm so honored to be a part. Growing up in Devereux has many wonderful memories enjoyed by all, and many more to come. Thanks, Ken. –**Brad Mills**, *long-time Devereux resident.*

The Author's Other Works

1. *Rabbit Row: The Life and Times of J.P. Mitchell*, KM&A Press, Springfield, IL, 2004, 372 pages

2. *Sister Raphael: The Personal and Family History of Jennie Roscetti Mitchell*, KM&A Publishing, Springfield, IL, 2006, 290 pages

3. *In the Bonds: Fraternity Life in the '60s,* Seagull Press, Springfield, IL, 2009, 352 pages

4. *North-End Pride: The Story of Lanphier High School, Its People and Community,* Seagull Press, Springfield, IL, 2014, 352 pages

5. *We Band of Brothers: The First 100 Years of Illinois Delta Chapter of ΣAE, Vol. I,* Seagull Press, Springfield, IL, 2013, 284 pages

6. Funny You Should Ask: A Memoir, Seagull Press, Springfield, IL, 2017, 269 pages

7. *My Working Life: Finding Meaning through Twists and Turns,* Seagull Press, Springfield, IL, 2016, 176 pages

8. *Bits and Pieces of My Life: A Memoir*, Seagull Press, Springfield, IL, 2017, 233 pages

9. *My Friend Bunk: Hubert A. "Bunk" Douglas*, KM&A Publishing, Springfield, IL, 2009, 58 pages

10. *Converse Kids: Growing Up in the '50s*, Seagull Press, Springfield, IL, 2009, 41 pages

11. *At the Top of My Game: My Five Years in the Life Insurance Business,* Seagull Press, Springfield, IL, 2011, 105 pages

12. *Our Seasons in the Sun: A High School Memoir*, Seagull Press, Springfield, IL, 2017, 222 pages

13. *A Glimpse into a Life: Merle A. Douglas*, Seagull Press, Springfield, IL, 2016, 70 pages

14. *Living Your Legacy Writing Kit: How to Record and Publish Your Personal Story or Family History*, Seagull Press, Springfield, IL, 2008, 44 pages

15. *My Buddy Joe*, Seagull Press, Springfield, IL, 2019, 99 pages

Some of these books can be obtained from the author's website, www.KenMitchellBooks.com.

I want to turn the clock back to when people lived in small villages and took care of each other.
--Pete Seeger

In Memory of

Leanne Bedolli

Dominic C. Giacomini

Dedicated to My Friend

Dominic C. Giacomini
Who Made This Book Possible

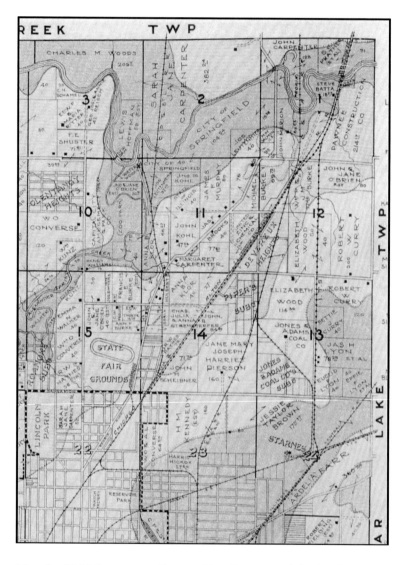

Map 1. 1914 Sangamon County Plat. Devereux is in Sections
11& 12. Much of it is in Capital Township. (Courtesy of the
Sangamon Valley Collection of the Lincoln Library

Table of Contents

Foreword

Preface

Introduction

Conclusion

Afterword

Acknowledgements

Appendix

About the Author

Elenore "Rudy" (Rodolfi) Rudolph

Foreword

It all started with softball, my entry into the Springfield Sports Hall of Fame, and our mutual friend, Art Spiegel. Art put me in touch with Ken Mitchell, author of a wonderful book *North-end Pride: The Story of Lanphier High School, Its People and Community.* I shared with Ken my pride in Springfield's North End through stories of my Italian immigrant parents and growing-up in the predominantly Italian and Polish Devereux Heights.

Looking back now, at 91 years old, perhaps the last remaining child of those first immigrants, I see the community for the very special place it was. Ken has brought our little village, its people and their customs and habits to life again with his retelling of our story.

I've learned things about the founding that I never knew. Perhaps the community's unique beginnings explain its cohesiveness, built on shared family values and hard work. We lived as one big family. Everybody helped everybody. It was fun for me to go back in time and relive my memories of people and places now gone. It was a great experience growing up there and thanks to Ken, others can appreciate its history too.

Elenore "Rudy" (Rodolfi) Rudolph

July 11, 2019
East Peoria, Illinois

Village is a place where you can find peace, unity, strength, inspiration and most importantly a natural and beautiful life" — Minahil urfan

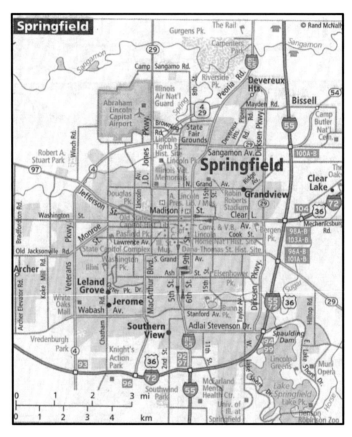

Map 2. Even Rand McNally points out in bold print the Village of Devereux Heights in the north-end corner of Springfield, IL. (*Rand McNally 2020 Road Atlas*, p. 73)

Preface

How this book came about is a story in itself. When I wrote *North-End Pride*, the history of Springfield's blue collar, working class neighborhoods, I mentioned what little I could find about many of the other mini-communities that grew up and enriched this city of Lincoln's.

The strange thing is that there was not much about them even in the Sangamon Valley Collection, that part of the city's library dedicated to local history. I thought to myself that I might return some day and research some of those other gems. Well, I was busy with other writing projects, so this rewarding project was postponed.

Until now. This almost forgotten Village of Devereux Heights has now come to light, as it should.

Three years ago I delivered one of my *North-End Pride* books to a fellow on Lake Springfield. While chatting in his front room and looking out over the blue water, Dominic Giacomini told me how he spent the first twelve years of his life in Devereux Heights. After reminiscing happily about that long-ago time in that small village, he sat up and said, "Hey, Ken, if you're interested, let me show you around out there some time."

I reminded myself of my commitment to study some of those small communities I had briefly discussed in my book four years before. I took "Nick" up on it and we met in front of the Jailhouse Tavern the next week. I drove around some of the streets as Nick told me bits and pieces about the history of Devereux and some of his fond memories.

The first contacts Nick introduced me to were the Yoggersts. Bob and Mary live at the end of Angelo Street, near where her grandparents once lived. They were part of the Golab family, some of the early pioneers who made that far-out place their home.

A week later, I called on a childhood friend of mine whose family had roots in Devereux. Tom Blasko had built a nice home on West Street in the village. I visited with him and his wife Betty Jo (Feleccia), who graduated one year ahead of me at Lanphier High. Tom gave me a quick sketch of who lived where in the early days of Devereux.

With several people the Yoggersts and Blaskos provided me, I was ready for one-on-one interviews to begin researching Devereux.

I decided to gather enough information to submit an article to one of the newspapers in town. There certainly was not enough material for anything close to a book, I figured.

That was in February 2016.

This little project then stalled in favor of three memoirs I wrote that spring and summer. Unfortunately, when I reconnected with the Devereux Project this spring, two of my oldest resources had passed away and a third now had memory problems. That wasn't smart on my part. One of the most important lessons I teach in my workshop on writing memoirs and family stories is to interview the oldest people first. I failed my own core principle.

But there were plenty of other not-as-old people to see and talk with, so I began anew and what you have in your hands is indeed a book, not just an article. I *was* able to gather enough material to give you a short history of this fascinating "little village that could." I borrowed my title from *The Little Engine That Could* because this village exemplifies those same two core values as Watty Piper's American fairytale does: optimism and hard work.

I felt I had a real connection with these folks, as they told me about their fathers and grandfathers working in the mines. I come from a family of a grandfather and uncles who worked the mines. There were many similar elements that I could relate to. And I think those aspects helped spur me on and helped me become excited about these village people and their lifestyle.

My mother's people are Italians (which most of Devereux was at its beginning). Mom grew up in Starnes, an even smaller mining town, sandwiched between what is now Northgate and Grandview Village. All the 23 families there were Italian save one German and one Polish, my mother told me. My grandfather was a Roscetti from Calasico, Italy and my grandmother was an Antonacci from LaRocca, just up the hill from Calascio. (Miraculously, they met in the States, never knowing each other in the Old Country.)

They eventually moved to Converse Avenue, just east of 19th Street, so as a child I was at my grandparents' house every day, sometimes twice a day. I grew up eating all that great "Dago" food. I would open the back door to their kitchen and immediately smell pasta simmering on Grandma's Detroit Jewel stove. I would sometimes be asked to retrieve from the pantry the gallon tin of Partanna Extra Virgin Olive Oil for Grandma. I could not help but look up at the sausages drying from the rafters. Were they delicious with Grandpa's homemade wine and assorted cheeses!

I have spent the last few months interviewing and researching the very same kind of people my grandparents were. After all, they are my people too. I asked them as many questions as I could think of to find out every part of the Devereux story. Obtaining pictures was more of a challenge; I wish I had more—but 50 isn't too bad. As in most history books, the writing is the easy part. I finished the first draft in early June and asked some of my new village friends to review it and correct what I got wrong.

I was committed to not allowing this village and its people and their story to die. To that end, if nothing else, I feel I have succeeded.

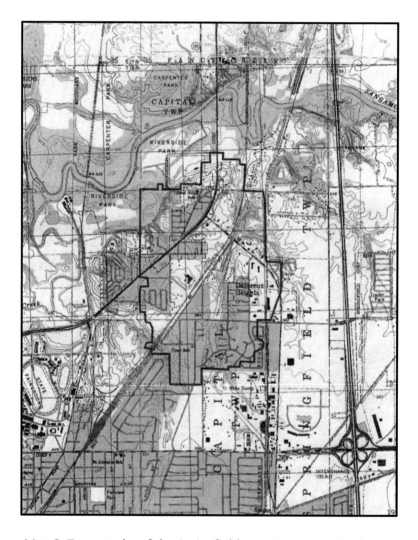

Map 3. Topography of the Springfield area. Devereux Heights is near the center. It may be kind of hard to see those wiggly lines that show variations in elevation. Contours galore punctuate the village of Devereux. (Sangamon County Planning Commission)

Introduction

Blue collar. People helping each other. Building houses together. Celebrating together. Making wine together. Grieving together.

These are things people in the small village of Devereux Heights, on the very north edge of Springfield, were known for, going back to 1913 (and even before) when people began buying lots there.

"Devereux" is the very north end of the North End of Springfield, IL. Everything the North End is known for— loyal, community-minded, God-fearing, country-loving, hard-working, frugal—Devereux is that and more.

Long considered an enclave, an outpost, an "out in the sticks" shirttail cousin of Springfield, Devereux is anything but that nowadays. It has legitimacy, reputation, and values other Springfieldians would envy. (And now it has its own book and history lesson.)

Honestly, I was expecting run-down houses, poor self-esteem, an out-of-touch attitude, and a backwardness. My only connection with it had been growing up on the North End and attending grade school with some Devereux kids.

Once I began going out there, driving around, talking to people, and exploring the rich history of the hamlet, I was impressed. It was nothing like I had thought it would be. There are really nice houses on large, spacious lots. The people are friendly and respectful—although a little cautious until they trust you. It is vibrant and optimistic.

As I slowly drove down each and every one of the 15 streets in the village, I thought to myself, "I wouldn't mind living here." There is an immediate atmosphere of friendliness and inclusiveness. I know that sounds Pollyanna, but it's the God's truth. You feel good just being in its orbit. Even "charming" is a word that might come to mind.

Being on the very tip of Springfield, you do get the feeling you are out a ways, but drive down the main east-west road, and you are at Wal-Mart's front doors in less than three minutes.

I've come to love, like, respect and appreciate this little village . . . its people and its rich history. Its pioneers were coal miners—immigrants who made their houses homes, their backyards food-producing, their children good citizens, and their country better.

You have in your hands the short history of a long-lived community. Enjoy it.

A village is a hive of glass, where nothing unobserved can pass.--Charles Spurgeon

The Irrepressible Harry H. Devereux

Chapter One

Harry H. Devereux

The story of the formation and development of the village of Devereux Heights, Illinois—and its unwillingness to shrink and die like many other coal mining "company towns"—really begins with the story of a remarkable man named Harry H. Devereux.

The official biographer of Harry H. Devereux, Joseph Wallace, in his 1904 book on the history of Sangamon County, together with numerous newspaper accounts, states he was born in Detroit, Michigan, on January 27, 1866. His mother moved young Harry to Springfield in the year 1871, when he was six years old.

A Mother's Passion

In fact, there is a much larger narrative here that took some time to unravel. His mother was Marie L. Devereux who was 26 and likely a widow when they moved to Springfield. There is no explanation why the young mother chose Springfield. But it must be a fact that she was smart, ambitious and resourceful—traits later ascribed to her son—because the single mother quickly established herself in a reasonably good job to raise Harry and give him a fighting chance in life. To that end, she was totally committed and successful.

She also must have been cunning enough—and/or attractive enough—to have somehow fought the odds and lifted herself into that rarified air of Springfield society. Within a few years in that environment she made the acquaintance of one of the city's most eligible bachelors, the widower Redick M. Ridgely, one of the 13 sons of the local tycoon Nicholas H. Ridgely.

It was in the capital city that his father, known as N.H. Ridgely, founded a number of businesses through his flagship enterprise, N.H. Ridgely & Company. Among them were the Ridgely National Bank, the Wabash Railroad, and farmland.

Redick, according to his biography, was principally a public servant most of his life, having held a number of positions within the city of Springfield government. He was a very active Democrat politician and obviously well-connected. (Curiously, the 1880 census lists his occupation as "grocer" in Chicago. Perhaps that was one of his family's profit centers, such as a wholesale foods company, under the N.H. Ridgely & Company umbrella.)

His first marriage in 1850 was to Margret Aitken, who was born in Scotland. Margret apparently died around 1874 (possibly in childbirth), after giving him four children: Alice M., Janey H., Redick, Jr., and John A.

Marrying Well

Unfortunately, we don't know the circumstances of how Marie and Redick met, but she "married well." The union took place at the first of the year, January 29, 1880, when she was 35 and he was 50. She instantly became the de facto mother of his four children: Alice, 16, Janey, 15?, Redick, 13, John, 8, and of course her beloved Harry, 16. As the manager of the household at Sixth and Allen Streets, Marie assumed the burden of those responsibilities. They were considerably lightened with the help of at least two servants, the Reis sisters, Minnie, 16, and Rosa, 19.

Even though Marie was past the ideal childbearing age of those days when she married Redick, it appears she had two more children of her own, another boy, William, and a girl, Mabel V. She likely raised those two children with some semblance of peace, as the older children were beginning to leave the nest to seek their own way in the world.

Once she had arrived in Springfield in 1871, Marie saw to it that young Harry received a good education, first in public schools, both elementary and high school. At one point, his biography states, he was a student at Andrew M. Brooks' school. It doesn't take much imagination to assume Mr. Ridgely, as Harry's mother's suitor and/or husband, placed him in that prestigious private school .

Keeping It All in the Family

Harry landed an entry-level job at the Ridgely National Bank in downtown Springfield as a messenger, possibly while still in school or right after graduation. His curiosity and natural business acumen propelled the young man to succeed at all costs. His biographer explains that, "Step by step [Devereux] was advanced to the position of paying teller, and continued that relationship with the bank for many years." It is more than likely that Harry's set of promotions were aided by his stepgrandfather, the family patriarch, who was president of the bank until his death in 1888.

Through love or expediency, or both, the Ridgely connection continued in Harry's life. At the age of 30, in 1895, it was greatly strengthened when he took for his wife, a certain Alice M. Ridgely, the daughter of R.M. Ridgely. They took up residence at 1218 S. 2nd Street. In other words, he married his stepsister!

Unfortunately, Alice died just three years later at age 33, probably in childbirth, leaving Harry with his namesake son, Harry H. Devereux II. Harry raised his son himself as a widower (probably with the help of an ample household of servants) for the next 17 years before remarrying.

He then took a second wife, Nell Selby, daughter of Mrs. Julia Selby, in 1915 (just a year after his dear mother passed). Nell had no children of her own during their marriage. Harry may have already known Nell before courting because she was an assistant secretary in the downtown office of the coal company he founded during that period and then managed. They lived at 1204 South Sixth Street, on what was called "Aristocracy Hill," because of the high-end houses that lined the tree-shaded streets south of the city center.

Harry's Political Career

Devereux had a natural affinity for people and politics. He was probably influenced and tutored along the way by his stepfather as he immersed himself in that rough and tumble world they both excelled at. Because of his many acquaintances through his position at the bank, in 1901 the 35-year-old Devereux ran for assistant county supervisor on the Democratic ticket. As a hard-working ward committeeman, he was the only Democrat elected from Capital Township that year.

Seeing him prove himself as electable and part of the system that ran things in those days, his party placed Devereux on the mayoral ballot two years later. He won election in 1903 by carrying every precinct except one. In 1905, the mayor was reelected for another two-year term.

At this point I must place Devereux's political career squarely in historical context. Springfield was notorious as a vice-ridden, racist, and corrupt city during this period. There are no two ways around it: it was rotten to the core. Devereux was, by virtue of his position and profession, in that core. The central part of town had a sleazy section called the levee district that symbolized Springfield's rottenness, rampant graft, and crime.

According to newspaper articles at the time, the politicians used that wonton lawlessness to elevate people like Devereux into power. Things actually deteriorated so far that even the Democratic Party lost trust in Devereux, even though they backed him in an unsuccessful third term attempt. His lack of appeal by both sides guaranteed the election of an independent candidate. (See the newspaper articles about this in the Appendix.)

It must be concluded that Devereux was so complicit in that cesspool of corruption that he must be viewed as a contributing factor leading to the 1908 Race Riot, which occurred just a year after he left office. The worst smear on our city's history, it resulted in the displacement of 2,000 black citizens by a mob of 5,000 European-Americans and European immigrants.

Participation Begets Prominence & Vice versa

Throughout his various career points in Springfield, Harry Devereux was immersed in all manner of other business and civic activities. How he found time to do them all is a testament to his tireless work ethic and skill in time management.

For example, he was treasurer of the Home Building and Loan Association and the American Southdown Breeders' Association. He also held membership in the Episcopal church and in several fraternal organizations, including the Court of Honor, Royal Circle, Loyal Americans, Modern Woodsmen of American, the Knights of the Maccabees and the Benevolent and Protective Order of Elks. Hopefully, he provided more help to his community in these than he did during his political life.

Harry H. Devereux Dies

Harry Devereux passed away at his home at 1317 Lowell Avenue on May 11, 1926 after an illness of eight months. He was sixty years old. His wife Nell predeceased him eight years earlier. He was survived by his son, Harry II, and grandson, Harry H. Devereux III, as well as several half-brothers and sisters. The city hall was closed on the afternoon of his funeral out of respect for the office he once held.

His Main Legacy

After his political career imploded, Harry H. Devereux stood up, brushed his embarrassment off and decided to concentrate on running the coal company he had started just before becoming mayor. He continued that effort of organizing and operating the Chicago-Springfield Coal Company north of Springfield, just beyond the city limits, until his death. That, in turn, resulted in the development of a little village on the north edge of Springfield that bears his name and ensures his most enduring legitimate legacy. That little village is the real story behind this book.

The only reproduction I found of the Chicago-Springfield Mine. (1913). It is from the Herman Pierik & Co. selling plat. (Courtesy Sangamon Valley Collection or SVC)

Chapter Two

The Chicago-Springfield Coal Company

If you study a large coal mine map of underground **Springfield, as well as Sangamon County, you will see a matrix of thousands of miles of coal mine tunnels crisscrossing the area.** (The only area not dug out is a several block square around the state capitol complex, to prevent government subsidence—of which we have enough already.)

On the north edge of the city, outside the then city limits, Harry Devereux and a group of investors chose to sink one more coal mine. The reason was profit. Sangamon County was at that time one of the most productive counties in Illinois for bituminous coal. He named his coal mine the Chicago-Springfield Coal Company, and it lay just south and east of where Route 66 Bypass [present day Dirksen Parkway and before that 31st Street] passed under the railroad viaduct. It then continued on to connect with Peoria Road and then Chicago. No remnants of the mine can be seen today. Hardly anyone alive even knows the mine's story and that includes most Devereuxites.

Prime Location

The "Devereux Mine," as the Chicago-Springfield Mine came to be called by locals, was built to be strategically located there because the Chicago & Alton belt line looping through the east side of Springfield (and up East Grand Avenue, now 19th Street) passed just east of the mine tipple. Its sister line of the same name ran through the center of Springfield and carried passengers to points north and eventually to Chicago. It ran parallel with the Interurban line for some distance. There is sometimes confusion because both railroad tracks were called the Chicago & Alton. The belt line was exclusively for freight, especially coal hopper cars that were loaded at the coal tipple, the tall structure we usually recognize as "coal mines" in old photographs. The passenger C & A track ran along the west boundary of what was to become the village of Devereux Heights a few years after the mine was built.

When I was a boy growing up on "the North End" in the 1950s, there were still several tipples around town (all inactive), such as the one at 11th and Black Avenue and the one on Walnut Street, just north of North Grand Avenue. In the early 1900s, there were dozens of coal mines in Springfield and throughout the rest of Sangamon County. There were several active mines surrounding the new Devereux Mine at the turn of the century. For instance, just north of it was Peabody #6, west was the Empire Mine, and southeast was the Jones & Adams. A little farther south was the inactive Springfield #3 Mine, at Starnes, a tiny mining town by comparison.

My mother grew up in Starnes (in the shadow of the tall slag pile) with the other 22 families that sent their kids to the two-room brick schoolhouse in the center. That little school is still (but barely) standing. [I describe that village in detail in my biography of my mother called *Sister Raphael: The Personal and Family History of Jennie Roscetti Mitchell (1909 –m). Like most of my books, it is available for reading at the Lincoln Library's Sangamon Valley Collection on the third floor and also in the Illinois State Historical Library.*]

Organizing and Building the Mine

In May 1902, Harry Devereux pulled together a group of men to organize and back his vision. The five principals he handpicked to join him were George A. Wood (treasurer), John H. McCreery (secretary), James A. Hall (comptroller), and two other directors, David Watson and Emanuel Salzenstein. Devereux was, of course, president. These men put up $150,000 or approximately $4,500,000 in today's dollars. My guess is that much of that capitalization was money borrowed, as smart men used (and still use) the OPM system, "other peoples' money." You can imagine that the Ridgely National Bank held some of the notes. The group was thus ready to begin building the facilities and shafts by the middle of the year.

The bulk of the investment was for the purchase of the coal rights and the cost of building the mine's main structures, its infrastructure (which included the two main shafts and many side tracks), and auxiliary buildings. The 150 acres of land was likely priced minimally because more than half of it was poor quality land with draws and ravines. Naturally, they needed to have significant reserves available too.

Here is how the *Illinois State Register* described the resulting process in its October 31, 1903 article entitled "Struck Fine Vein of Coal":

". . . in the intervening time (after May 1903), a matter of but six months, land was purchased, coal rights bought up, machinery and experienced men secured, and a shaft 9 by 17 feet dug in the ground to the depth of 215 feet, and now the company has a mine, which when all is completed, will be able to produce 2,000 tons of coal daily."

The article goes on to exclaim that the company worked at a feverish pace, overcoming obstacles such as "several strata of hard flintlike stone . . . and many other setbacks. For the undertaking the company had at its disposal 1,100 acres of coal rights and 150 acres of top ground." (The mine also may have dug an additional air shaft off of Interurban Avenue, just west of the mine about a quarter mile south of the Bypass, which a local called an "air pit." He said in the early '50s they dumped slag down the hole to cover it up for safety reasons.)

"In no time at all, the Devereux Mine [the article continued] was looking like a real operation, with ten four-room houses for miners with families, one 27-room boarding house for single workers, one engine house measuring 30- by 40-feet, and one 40- by 60-feet boiler room, for the hoist elevators. Two large Aetna engines were then installed, as well as two boilers with two more to follow."

Getting Down to Business

The following section is again directly taken from the above-mentioned article.

The digging started late in June [1903], *and since that time twenty-five men, all experienced miners, have been busily at work night and day turning up the dirt and blasting the rock. A large steam drill was used and at times it was found necessary to use dynamite. The men were used in three shifts, so that work has been going on practically every minute of the time since it was first started.*

After bringing up soft dirt for 17 feet, a layer of rock was struck, and this continued all the way down until the cap rock was reached only a few feet from the coal. There was a layer of cap rock five feet eight inches thick, which was hard as flint, and two men were kept busy all the time sharpening drills for the force at work, so hard was the rock. Under this was a layer of straight grain grey slate, two and one-half feet in thickness, and under this lay the coal, which was reached late Monday evening [October 26, 1903 after 5 months of non-stop digging and drilling].

The coal which has been taken out at this time, is said to be of the best quality. [Mine] Superintendent George Strebel says that it is excellent, and all of the members of the company are elated over the prospects. The work of opening up the new mine and working out the entries will begin at once, and it is the hope of the company to have the new coal on the market by the first of the coming year [1904].

The entries running from the bottom east and west will be twenty feet wide. The shaft itself will clear 8 by 16 feet after the timbers are placed in position, and this work will be started at once.

The location of the new mine is one of the best in the country. Right on the line of the railroad, the transportation facilities will be . . . first class. There will be 8,000 feet of side tracks and switches constructed at once in front of the mine; four 75 foot thick scales will be put in and the work on the top building of the mine will begin at once. Instead of *using steel for the construction of the top, the construction will be limited to wood as nearly as is practicable.*

Coal Production Readies and then Begins

The first official preview of how well the Chicago-Springfield Mine did during its building-up phase is summarized in the coal industry-friendly *1903 Annual Coal Report—New and Prospective Mines:*

A new shaft in Sangamon county, two miles north of the State Fairgrounds, is being sunk. It is on the line of the Chicago & Alton railroad. The name of the company is the Chicago and Springfield Coal company. This is a fine location for a shaft, and it is the intention of the owners to equip the plant in first-class style.

The *1904 Annual Coal Report—New Mines* portended an even more optimistic future:

The Chicago-Springfield Coal Co. has opened out a new mine on the line of the C & A railroad, two and one half miles north of the corporate limits of the village of Ridgely [the north part of Springfield], Sangamon county: the plant is first-class in every particular. The hoisting and air shafts are each 235 feet deep. The coal seam is No. 5 of the general section, and is six feet thick. The hoisting shaft is 8 x 10 feet in the clear and the air shaft is 8 x 20 feet; five feet of the air shaft is taken off of one end for a stairway and escapement.

A town site will soon be located, ten houses, with a hotel, have already been erected. The underground works are laid out on the most modern plan, and the coal will be worked on what is known as the panel system.

Historical Summary of Production

The Directory of Illinois Coal Mines (Sangamon County), 1993, Rev. 2009, gives an overview of Devereux's mine [Mine Index 3347] in terms of key elements, years of operation, production numbers, etc. Here are the main data, reorganized and restated:

1. Location: Township 16N Range 5W, Section 12, SW SW NW
2. Geology: Seams 230 feet deep, average thickness 6.2 feet, mining method: RPP (Room-and-pillar panel)
3. Total mined-out acreage: 907 acres.
4. Geologic Problems Reported: None
5. Production History: 4,305,164 tons
6. Years of Operation: 1904-1927

7.   Last Production Run: March 1927

It seems to the untrained eye that Harry Devereux could be proud of how well his mine did over its 23-year run. When I compared its statistics to other mines in the area, it was about average. (The 2,000 tons a day was an idealized projection. The mine actually yielded 800 tons a day, a little less than half that amount, which was still very good.)

And remember, Sangamon County coal production was among the best in the world. I don't know how well he and his fellow organizers came out financially, but my guess is that they each earned a bucket full of money. The same can't be said of the hundreds of coal miners whose daily labor helped make the investors substantial gains, and probably made the principals rich. Mining was a gruesome, dangerous and underpaid activity that poor immigrants signed up for because there were few other options.

Still, the miners earned enough to raise families and produce livelihoods commensurate with other low class families in Springfield.

A Miner's Life

The following section (and title heading) is taken directly from my biography about my mother, *Sister Raphael*.

A little aside: I called it that because Mom, against her Italian father's strong wishes, joined the Franciscan Order when she was 19 and took the name Raphael because he was the angel of healing in the Bible. She became a Registered Nurse and set up pediatric wards in several of the 3rd Order of St. Francis Hospitals. She was eventually overworked and run down and so decided to go home and recuperate. Her Mother Superior thought she wasn't coming back, so asked Rome to release her from her vows. She loved her eight years as a nun and never regretted joining. She was lucky to be a nun through most of the 1930 Depression years and never had to worry about where her next meal was coming from or where she would sleep the next night.

Since my grandfather, "Bert" Roscetti, and most of his sons went to the mines, I thought it would save me a lot of time just copying what I had spent weeks researching about mining and the men who did it, from my mom's book.

It is also germane because "Grandpa Bert" was a contemporary of many of the early miners at the Devereux mine, who were "the first generation in Devereux." He was born Berardino Carlo Roscetti in 1881 and came to America with his father in 1902. He moved to the Springfield area after mining in Windber, Pennsylvania for a few years. He then mined at Dawson, Jones & Adams, and later in life at Peabody #10, south 20 miles, near Kincaid, Illinois.

When they got to America—the saying goes— Italians learned three things: that the streets were not paved with gold; that the streets were not paved at all; and that they were expected to pave them! Thus, in 1890, most Italian Americans were working as laborers. The other most common occupation was in the trades and transportation, such as railroad workers, peddlers, etc. For thousands of Italians, the labor work they found plentiful was in the coal mines. Most all of my immigrant relatives were coal miners. The one I knew best was Grandpa.

My grandfather's face was riddled with about a dozen little bluish marks. When I was a small child I asked my mother what those were. "Those are scars from where Papa got hit with little pieces of coal when he worked in the mine," she said. *"The blue color is what was left from the coal material."* (It was actually the blue shale that impregnated the coal.) *Those marks fascinated me, and I asked Grandpa himself numerous times about them. He usually shrugged off the question by changing the subject as an object lesson for me, "From the coal mine. Hard work. You go to school, work with your head, not hands. Don't forget what I say,* capisce?"[1] *[He taught himself to read and write from newspapers and took pride in "never seeing a schoolteacher's face". My grandmother remained illiterate, except for counting money, which she excelled at.]*

I want to give you an idea what kind of work Grandpa had to put up with for over forty years in the mines. When he came to America at the beginning of the 20th century, he started working in the coal fields of Pennsylvania with his father, uncles, and other relatives. After four years, he moved to central Illinois to mine in Sangamon County. At the

Starnes Spfld. #3 Mine just north of present day Grandview. This is a typical configuration of mine tipples (wooden) in that era. (c.1885) (SVC)

time it was one of the top coal-producing counties in Illinois, which was the second leading coal-producing state in the country (after Pennsylvania).[2] There were approximately fifty coal mines in Sangamon County (and maybe twenty in and around Springfield proper) when Bert Roscetti came to Illinois. The reason so many Italians and other foreigners worked in the mines was because they couldn't find work anywhere else. Many of the immigrants had farming backgrounds but there were not enough farming jobs to go around. There were two other factors that sealed their fates in the mines: a language barrier and plain old prejudice against foreigners.

The following statement from Midnight at Noon, *by James Krohe Jr., describes what had become a common sight in Springfield. It gives a vivid recollection of what coal miners experienced on a daily basis.*

> *For eight months of the year, from September through April, these men can be seen daily on their way in the mornings to the various tipples which mark the entrances of the mines, and returning home late in the afternoons with blackened faces and grimy clothes that suggest something of the dingy realities of this underground occupation. Some of them had been digging and loading cars; others had been laying tracks, timbering passages, driving mule-drawn carts, or "trapping" (tending passage entries). The shot-firers begin their work at night when the others leave off; theirs is the dangerous task of handling explosives and blasting out walls of coal for the next day's work.[3]*

Early in the morning, my grandfather and the other miners clustered around the entrance to the main shaft with lunch buckets in hand. When the whistle blew at 7:00 a.m., the men started their eight to ten hours of backbreaking work, piling into caged elevators that carried fifteen or twenty of them down two hundred and fifty feet to the bottom. As they looked up at the sunlight that got fainter and smaller, they went past walls dripping with black water. Leaving the cage after their two-minute ride, the miners fanned out, most on mule-driven carts to the coal face, which was as long as two miles.

The mines were constructed like city blocks. There were main tunnels, also called "entries," running horizontally, from which series of "rooms" would run perpendicularly. The rooms were twenty-five feet wide and as high as the seam was thick, usually five feet or so. The miners would dig coal back into the room they were carving out, as far as they could go, many times 250 to 300 feet deep.

I don't know what kind of jobs my grandfather had over his career, but Mom said he spent most of his time shoveling coal into carts. This was usually done with one or two partners. They would load the carts all day long with football-size chunks of coal. Paid only for loaded coal, a strong miner working a good seam could load four or five tons a day, and he sweated for every pound of it. Here is how one miner lamented the daily grind, quoted again from Krohe's excellent little book on Illinois coal:

> The actual loading of the coal was only part of your day's work. All this other stuff you handled—like slate and sulfur and rock that came with the coal—you had to throw back into the "gob" for which you got paid nothing. It was no place for the weak or timid.

This was my grandfather's life's work: crouching in the dim light of the carbide lamps for those long hours. Think of all that dust he was breathing in. Besides the coal dust that caused debilitating "black lung disease" in thousands of miners [like himself], there were other, more immediate risks to coal miners. Although they were rare, explosions could occur from methane gas combusting with the flame from the carbide lamps the miners had to use. Cave-ins were the most terrifying concern of miners. Grandfather and *every other miner kept an ear cocked for the unmistakable creaking sounds of a roof about to give way. Carbon monoxide—the "black damp"—could suffocate a man in minutes. Also heavily laden coal cars rolling through dimly lit tunnels were often fatal traps for the careless. Here's how one miner remembers the risk-reward bargain they all made:*

> *There was so many ways you could get hurt in coal mining; it was different than anything else. There were two things you had to do. First, you had to take care of yourself, and then you had to learn your job. 'Cause if you didn't learn to take care of yourself, you didn't need any job, 'cause you weren't going to have any. [4]*

My mother told me Grandpa got hurt many times but never a real serious injury like a broken leg. Nor was he involved in any serious cave-ins or explosions. The only accident that was fairly serious was when his back and shoulders were hurt from a large piece of slate that fell from the roof.

Working in one of the most dangerous jobs, my grandfather raised a family of seven kids and a wife on about $5.00 a day, sometimes $7 or $8 a day. (That was based on between 57¢ to $1.27 per ton in 1914.) With those wages, he may have earned as much as $2,000 some years. However, with the summer layoffs, overproduction and occasional strikes, many miners earned less than $600 a year. (In the 1910 Census, it says he was out of work for 16 weeks the previous year; that sounds like the summer hiatus.)

For example, in 1932, when union problems culminated in Sangamon County, there were 20 major shipping mines. Workers in nine of them didn't work a single day that year, and of the other eleven, they averaged only 91 days the whole year! You can see why my grandfather worked alongside many of his fellow miners laying riprap around the shoreline of the newly formed Lake Springfield as part of the Works Progress Administration (WPA) project during those early years of the Depression. Another WPA project Bert Roscetti worked on, Mom recalls, was at the Fairgrounds. She doesn't know what it was exactly; my guess is that he helped build some of the buildings still standing today. That's when most of them were built, like the Exposition Building and Grandstand.

Growing up, I heard my grandfather sing the praises of John L. Lewis, the founder and president of the powerful United Mine Workers of America. He felt that the bushy eye-browed Lewis, whom he knew personally, saved the miners. However, if you read the history of the Miners' Wars of the 1930s in Illinois, it would be easy to take Lewis to task for reducing the miners per day wage from $7.50 to $5.00 during that decade. That's pretty much what my grandfather was earning twenty years before.

Mom's cousin, Hugo Antonacci, recalls [in his memoir that I edited] vividly how his family was threatened when his father broke through the picket lines to feed his large family. The boys had to stay up all night with guns pointing out the windows to fend off men with Molotov cocktails from burning down their house. He and his brothers then had to go to school the next day. (Bill Ranalletta, whose family lived behind the Antonaccis, told me that the strikers in fact threw a bomb at the Antonacci house.)

I didn't personally see any of my uncles come home from the mine, but my cousin Bernie described his dad's *procedure when he returned home. (Since that time—in the 1950s—I believe miners wash and change at the mine before returning home.)*

> *I recall when I was a youngster seeing him come home from the mine, caked in the black soot, with only his eyes and teeth shining white in the dark mask. He also carried that round cylinder of a lunch bucket, with a handle and a couple of sections that stacked one upon another. I also recall the first thing he would do is go down to the basement where he had installed a rudimentary shower and spend a half hour scrubbing off the grime after coming home from the mine.*

Doesn't that sound like a pretty miserable existence? That kind of working life was the daily ritual of most of Devereux's family men. They were hardy souls and put up with it for decades, ruining their bodies in the process. It was staple talk around our supper table during my younger years discussing who had black lung, what lawyers (Dad called them "mouthpieces") did the best job representing the miners, and how much administrative judges finally gave them in restitution.

Dominic Giacomini, after reading this section, relates what his mother, Rosie, recalls of her dad and his work in the mines:

My dad would walk home after mining coal all day, covered with black coal dust, and he couldn't wait for his evening meal with his family. However, he was so tired he'd fall asleep at the table.

Devereux Mine Calls It A Day

Coal mines sometimes ran their course when seams of coal became thinner and/or more difficult to access. In those cases, the cost of labor would begin to exceed the cost of production. There were other macro-economic factors at play. One was "that trains moved from coal to diesel," according to Curtis Mann, director of the Lincoln Library's local history department, called Sangamon Valley Collection.

Devereux Mine fit into that same mold that eventually caught most mines in Sangamon County, which had been the most productive county in all of Illinois. But, it had been a good run and held its own relative to other area mines. Here are facts to support that statement.

According to the *Illinois Coal Reports*, which kept such statistics and more, Chicago-Springfield Coal Mine in 1906 (just two years into production) ranked 15th in Sangamon County for output. In 1914 it was ranked 13th out of 31 mines in the county for output and 29th in the state for mines that delivered between 100,000 and 200,000 tons in the year. In 1921 it ranked 18th of 29 mines in the county for output.

Harry Devereux and his board of directors were savvy businessmen who studied these trends in the coal industry. Management understood those trends were not in their favor. They noticed, for example, as James Krohe Jr. points out in his book, *Midnight at Noon*, that two trends boded poorly for continued coal dominance in Sangamon County and for their mine in particular. One was that machines were fast replacing picks and shovels. Second, strip mining was on the rise in Illinois, which required "fewer men than even mechanized shaft mining and further spared the owners the necessity of providing elaborate and expensive ventilation, haulage, and safety equipment."

When the owners decided to stop the production and close down the mine in the spring of 1927, the attendant structures were likely torn down within a relatively short time to prevent lawsuits for trespass, attractive nuisance, negligence, and other torts. When Rudy Rodolfi was a small child (born in 1928), she recalls seeing and playing near the slag pile ("not nearly as large as the one at Jones & Adams") at the north end of Devereux. "There was nothing left except that big hill." She's the only living village elder who saw or remembers the mine or its aftermath.

She does recall that the freight train track serving the old mine was still firmly in place—tracks, ties, spikes, and all. "Betty Golab and I would walk that track from school to eat lunch at our homes and then walk it back."

Jim Bartlett, a few years younger than Rudy, told me, "those tracks were gone when I was a child growing up in the mid-'30s. All that remained from Mayden Avenue north was the railway bed that hugs the west side of the gully." He expanded that thought:

Those tracks were still intact south of Mayden while I grew up. As a matter of fact, the Jones & Adams mine used those tracks to park hopper cars full of coal in the area now part of Twin Lakes. I used to go over to those cars, like other kids, and take coal home. Years later, they were removed when the mine quit operation due to a fire they couldn't put out.

Brad Mills remembers the south tracks intact when he grew up in the early '60s.

They ran parallel to Piper Road and east of it. They were still intact because we used to walk on them on the way home from St. Al's.

A Long-forgotten Bridge

Rudy also relates that there was a bridge across that track a couple blocks south of the mine. It went over North Street (today Randy Street) to allow pedestrians, bikes and (the few) motor vehicles to move freely from West Devereux to East Devereux, terms probably never used by the locals. At that time, North Street went through the entire addition, from Interurban Avenue to East Street. That's the first time anybody had mentioned that bridge to me—thank goodness for Rudy and her great memory! I also discovered the reference of that bridge in one of the land transfers I looked at. I would love to have a picture of that connecting link, but I doubt it was ever taken in those hard days and years. All she recalled was that "it was wooden without sides or railings, plus some metal on it." I placed a picture in the Appendix section at the end of the book that appears similar to that description minus the metal components. My guess is that it spanned the ravine at around 100 feet in length. The ravine was deep enough there that the train could easily pass under it.

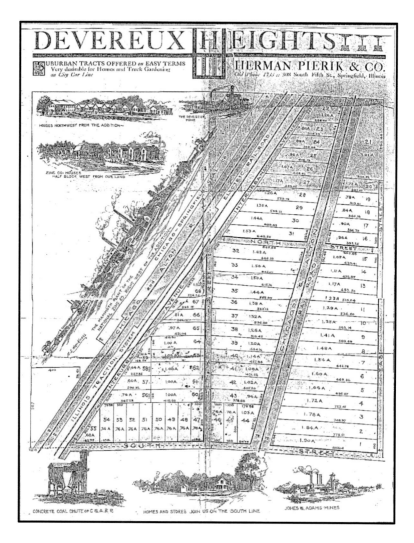

Sales Plat of Devereux Heights. It shows the five original roads:
Interurban Ave, South St., East St., North St. & Central St. 1913.
(Courtesy SVC.)

Chapter Three

A Town in the Making

According to the internet's Wikipedia website, "a company town is a place where practically all stores and housing are owned by the one company that is also the main employer. Company towns are often planned with a suite of amenities such as stores, churches, schools, markets and recreation facilities."

Mining companies sometimes configured an actual town near their mines that would supply its workforce in exchange for the amenities to the miners and their families mentioned in the above definition. The town that sprang up near the Devereux Mine never fit that tight definition. However, it was Mr. Devereux's intention all along to create a contiguous town where his employees and workers would live.

His idea was more on the lines of another source of income, in addition to captured capital. In his delightful and detailed memoir penned in 1999 (*A History of My Life—As I Remember It*), Merino Giacomini puts it more bluntly:

[Devereaux Heights] "was nothing more than a mining camp. It was named for the owner of the coal mine who also conveniently owned a sizable spread of land adjacent to his mine. My father [Constantino], like many of the other miners, was coerced into buying a building lot from Mr. Devereaux in order to obtain a job in his coal mine."

What's in a Name?

As a note of clarification, the name "Devereux" is the formal spelling usually preferred. As you can see from Mr. Giacomini's quote, it was often spelled like the French word, with the addition of the letter "a." Again, referring to Wikipedia, which should not necessarily be taken as authority, "Devereaux is a variation of the surname Devereux based on the common English mispronunciation 'Devero'. . . Devereux is a surname of Norman origin frequent in England and the English-speaking world." I will continue to use the spelling which Mr. Devereux used for his name. Also, the word is informally pronounced "Dev-row," with just two syllables.

When I was growing up on the North End and attended St. Aloysius Grade School where lots of Devereux kids attended, we called Devereux Heights "Devereux," using the shortened version, never its formal name.

Devereux Heights

One would have to read his mind to determine Mr. Devereux's motive behind his real intentions, but it is true that he purchased much more land that was necessary if he were simply interested in building the requisite coal mine site, which took up just 3.01 acres. While the newspaper article in the previous chapter noted the mining company purchased 150 acres of "top land," a plat map surveyed and then recorded on May 17, 1913 measures a square parcel 2,400 feet on a side, or a net of 132.23 acres. Estimating (rather crudely using a rule) that about a third of that land was subtracted for transfer (to "National Zinc Company" across the tracks), railroad rights-of-way, and the coal mine itself, his development (today it would be called a subdivision), which he called "Devereux Heights," was around 76 acres, including streets. (See accompanying picture of the plat.)

There was a total of 68 lots in the original plat, which was a triangle configuration with the top cut off. The lot sizes were generous, many containing an acre or more. A subsequent sales sheet made use of a well-chosen USP (unique selling proposition): "You can get an acre lot for what a standard lot in the city would cost." Of course, in those days, most people—or at least most immigrants— would need a large kitchen garden plus a little grazing land for a cow, goats and chickens, for their large families of 5 to 10 children. So coerced or not, these lots were attractive to many miners.

The perimeter boundaries of the development project, including the mine, were the Chicago & Alton (passenger) Railroad on the west (the hypotenuse of the triangle), an east-west line just south of U.S. Route 66 Bypass on the north, East Street on the east, and South Street on the south. Bisecting the development on a slight angle to the right was the Chicago & Alton (freight) Railroad, which picked up the coal at the mine's tipple, at the north. If you look at the plat map at the beginning of this chapter, you will see Lot 21 at the very top right. That would have likely been 3.01 acres for the mine structures. Below it is Lot 20, 0.72 acres, which I'm guessing is where the company placed the miners' boarding house and some of the ten family houses.

There was a total of five streets initially connecting the three rows of lots: Interurban Avenue, South Street, Center Street, North Street, and East Street.

It lay in No-man's Land

The new settlement carved out of rough land with ridges, ravines, hills, and some flat spaces was not part of Springfield or even the northern most village contiguous with Springfield, called Ridgely. Technically, it was an unincorporated legal entity that remained so until 1967 when most of it was annexed into the capital city. It was originally serviced by the Sangamon County Sheriff's Department. For fire service, the resourceful denizens knew they were pretty much on their own, as a fire would have burned a house down by the time a fire brigade from town would have made it there. Even if they could get there at a reasonable time, there was no water service. I could find no evidence that any house had burned down in a fire.

If you take a look at the enclosed topography map, you will immediately wonder how in the world a surveyor was able to work a housing addition into those 76 acres.

43

There are several draws or ravines crisscrossing the plat, the most prominent ran on a slight angle through the middle, next to the freight tracks. Topo maps also display the "above sea level" measurement at 581 feet for the land around Devereux but as low as 560 feet at the bottom of the main ravine, and not much different in some of the other draws. I'm sure Mr. Devereux and his men were able to get that part of the land very cheap indeed. But, it worked out, and there are around 100-plus, happy families living and enjoying themselves and their neighbors in that enclave that now has a written history.

Mr. Hall is the Promoter

Once the coal mine was humming along, producing a prodigious amount of bituminous or soft coal, the powers-that-be decided it was time to fill up the rest of those 76 acres to the south with growing families which would further supply the human capital for their operation.

It is interesting to note that the development plat mentions in the certification portion at the bottom of the document that "we James A. Hall and Ema H. Hall his wife, proprietors of the above entitled DEVEREUX HEIGHTS, do hereby adopt, ratify and confirm the above plat and certificate of survey . . ." followed by more legalese stating it meets state law. The point is that this is surely the same James A. Hall who was the comptroller of the Chicago-Springfield Mining Co. My take on this is that Devereux appointed the Halls "proprietors," which usually means owners. In this case I believe it is used as meaning they "have an interest (such as control or present use) less than absolute and exclusive right," according to the *Merriam-Webster's Dictionary*. In other words, Devereux appointed one of his board members to be in charge of the surveying and platting of the development for a fee or commission. He either delegated this duty to Hall to reduce his own workload and/or to ensure an arm's length transaction for one reason or another, but it was a temporary arrangement.

Selling the Dream

Nine years after the mine began production and just three months after the plat was certified, Devereux, through his surrogates, put the lots up for sale. He chose a friend as his selling broker. His name was Herman Pierik and he ran a real estate brokerage firm in the city.

Pierik was picked because of his prominence in the city beyond his brokerage firm. He was a distinguished banker connected to the Jacob Bunn (private) Bank. He was also president of the Home Building & Loan Association, where Devereux also had worked. Devereux picked one of the best businessman in the city to represent his addition. He was also a trusted colleague at the HB&LA.

Transfer No. 31 in the Abstract of Title for part of Lot 43 (loaned to me by the Bartletts) contains a contract from the organizers *and Pierik* to Mr. Devereux "to have the exclusive right to handle, plat and sell all that part of the 76 acres, excepting railroad right of ways, dated May 1, 1913. Devereux, as owner, wanted to make sure he had the final say in selling the addition's lots.

However, five years later, on February 14, 1918, Devereux and his wife, Nelle, divested their interest in "all Lots 1 – 68" by deed to Mr. Pierik. I'm not sure why that reversal occurred. One would assume that many of the lots had sold, but the remaining ones were Pierik's to sell and profit by. (An interesting fact turned up later in the Abstract: In 1935 Pierik went bankrupt during the Great

Depression, losing the balance of his interest in Devereux Heights.)

Come and Get 'Em

The first offering of property for sale in Devereux that I discovered (via Stephanie at the Sangamon Valley Collection) was a classified ad in the local *Illinois State Register's* September 7, 1913 edition. There were actually ten real estate ads in that FOR SALE advertisement that day. The top and bottom ads pertained to the settlement south of the mine. (The others were land in the city of Springfield.) The first ad read:

> **A beautiful new house, just completed, and three acres of land with it, located [in the] north part of the city on street car line, $2500; cash $500, balance $20 monthly payments**

This small classified ad tells us several things. First, the listing agents at the bottom of the ad were Charles G. Wineteer and James A. Hall, working under the auspices of Herman Pierik, the broker in charge. So Hall again was directly involved in the offering, which was at first his charge from Devereux. Second, the ad also suggests the

47

house on the 3-acre tract was "a spec house," that is, built on the hope or speculation the owner would sell it, as opposed to a "contract house" for a party who had already purchased the property and hired a contractor to build a dwelling on it.

This makes sense because that is a common way to get a development off the ground: put up several spec houses first to show it's a thriving enterprise. Third, there were three obvious benefits for buyers in the ad: close to the Interurban (called "a streetcar line"), a very large (3 acre) property, and good terms of sale. Fourth, the ad implies that one acre lots, which were the normal unimproved property offerings, would be considerably cheaper. The listing at the bottom of the ad is different:

> **DEVEREUX HEIGHTS. Located near United Zinc & Chemical Co., Chicago-Springfield, Jones & Adams and Peabody mines, on car line. Choice acre tracts for sale on easy terms.**

It tells the readers that there is a newly available development for sale, adding the word "Heights" to make it sound classy. The property is close to a new Springfield employer, a zinc smelter operation, just west, across the railroad tracks and the Interurban (which ran parallel to the passenger railroad). Such smelters would employ lots of workers who would like to walk just a short distance to work. The ad also tells prospective buyers that the lots are near several area coal mines, also within walking distance.

I recall my grandfather telling me he walked to Jones & Adams Mine from his home in Starnes, about a mile south of that mine. That's just a 30-minute walk to work, crossing the cornfield Mr. Ford farmed (and sold to Gail Wanless in 1930 who leased it to George Handley), now Northgate Subdivision. Walking back home after a backbreaking day at the mine was probably longer and harder.

The *Illinois State Register* ran formal advertisements like the following display ad in its March 23, 1914 edition, probably on a regular basis:

ACRE TRACTS
Devereux Heights
Acre tracts offered on easy terms. Very fine for home and truck gardening.
Located northeast part of city on city car line.
We will sell you an acre of land for the price you pay for one cheap city lot.

HERMAN PIERIK & CO. 308 South 5ᵗʰ Street
Old Phone 1733

The next item I found in the local paper related to the Devereux parcels was dated two years later, March 25, 1915. It was under a classified ad in the Legal Section of the paper. This particular ad's heading in bold print read REALTY TRANSFERS. Out of the nine transfers, here was one that caught my eye:

Devereux, Harry H. et al. to
Steve Olsak, lot 35 Devereux
Heights addition;
consideration $1.

It verifies that Mr. Devereux owned this 1.44 acre lot (in the middle of his development) outright. The reference to the consideration being only $1 is a common method of stating that the value was agreed upon but not listed for privacy. One can always estimate the price at the Recorder of Deeds office, by counting up the revenue stamps on the deed document.

Thus, Devereux Heights was born and continued to develop, lot by lot. My guess is that most of the lots had been sold by the time the Depression hit in 1930. Of course, a number of homeowners likely did not weather that storm.

There were probably sales and resales and foreclosures. But in the end, Devereux, "the little village that could," stayed on a firm footing as a self-contained community of mainly Italians and then eventually diversified ethnically into the thriving village it is today.

Layout of Village Streets

Through ingenuity brought about by adding and reconfiguring streets, plus a little expansion to the south, Devereux Heights today has a total of 15 streets, from the original five. Explaining Devereux's street matrix can sound somewhat complicated without a map at hand.

The first major change in street configuration was eliminating most of East Street in favor of a street about 200 feet to the west. The owners early on decided to bisect the East Street lots almost in half to double the number of lots on what informally became known as "Dago Hill" Road. This switcheroo thus relegated the former East Street to an alleyway, except for a block-long section off of East Randy Street. That shortened East Street made a sharp turn to the north for a block and abruptly ended, where it would have gone directly into the mine property (and later to the Roll Inn). Where Randy Street started again, east of the ravine, a lane later called Magdalena Street continued as a very short (50 feet or so) twist to the north, accommodating just one house (Charlie Bedolli's, currently.)

As time went on, Devereux Heights expanded in the only direction it could, southernly, in what had been platted as Piper Subdivision. John H. Piper bought the land in late 1908 and was selling lots to people the following year in 1909, getting a strategic jump on Devereux by four years.

Mr. Piper saw the opportunity and moved on it fast. He understood that the new settlement of Devereux was going to expand along Piper Road. And it did expand early on and began sprouting houses on both sides from South Street (Mayden Avenue) down a few blocks, giving rise eventually to side streets Ida Mae Lane, Willow Lane, Vincent Street, Neil Road, and even a few houses on Hedge Lane Road, near Peabody #59 Mine, on its way to Sangamon Avenue.

Interurban Avenue later continued south from Mayden until it stopped a quarter mile down, populating around a dozen houses on that dead-end street. Finally, a new road, West Street, grew south off of West Mayden (and west of Piper) until it stopped at Neil Road, where the K.C.'s property lies today.

From now on, I will usually refer to the streets by their new names, even when I may be talking about people or events a long time ago. The street renaming process occurring in 1967 as a result of annexation will be revisited in the last chapter.

"Little Boxes, Little Boxes . . ."

While the addition was not exactly a company town as I mentioned at the onset of this chapter, it had one component that showed the mining company had a lot to say about the miners' lives and where they would reside. C-S Mining Company definitely put pressure on its miners to purchase homes in its new "Devereux Heights."

Rudy Rodolfi, whom I introduced in Chapter Two, told me that the mine "coerced" her father into purchasing a lot and then a house to place on the lot. (Merino Giacomini used that same harsh verb at the beginning of the chapter.) She described the house as having decent material and construction, but not great. That reminded me of the "Little Boxes" song written by Malvina Reynolds in which she uses the derisive term for suburban sprawl construction as "ticky-tacky." Here is Rudy describing her parents' meager house:

When my folks moved into their house [on Lot 10] on Angelo Street, it was just like most all the others in the neighborhood. They were called "Four-Room Houses" because they were small and square with two bedrooms next to the other on the left side and what you might call a living room/dining room on the right side with a kitchen behind it. Very simple. They had the distinctive hip roof, a simple porch, and, for some reason, two front doors. I never understood the need for an entrance into the front bedroom. Strange.

We also had a full basement where we stored canned food, hung up hams and sausage, and placed the four barrels for wine. Dad almost immediately built two rooms onto the back of the house. One was another bedroom for him and Joe to sleep in. The other room was a laundry room where Mom had her old, gray, square Maytag washing machine. He didn't finish off those rooms; they just had lathe on the walls.

We had no telephone until after I left home in '46 — or maybe a couple of years before. We did have a potbelly heating stove in the corner of the living room and a cooking stove in the kitchen, both with coal fuel. Dad had a small coal storage area in the basement. He bought the coal from the mine where he worked. We didn't get a furnace until Mary and I left home.

For some reason, we didn't have a cistern for our water supply. We just had 50-gallon barrels that caught rain water from the downspouts and used that for washing hair, taking baths and such. Our well was for drinking water. I remember it had a sack under the spout with salt in it to catch small white worms and centipedes and such. That was our water filtration system! We changed it every week or two. Before we got an icebox (in the early '40s), Dad would have a cement sack he would hoist down into the water to keep milk and butter and probably his beer cool in the summer.

The front yard wasn't very deep, and many families had picket fences. There was usually a long, crude bench in front of the fence where women might congregate in the evenings. For some reason, we never had one. [More on the front yard bench camaraderie in Chapter Six.]

Long-time pipefitter and resident of Devereux, Bob Yoggerst, observed that "another thing you notice about [some of] these houses is the first room you walked into was the kitchen." He explained that his house was and is still like that. He surmised that it had the big kitchen stove that helped reduce the cold chill when the door was opened, since the other doors leading into the bedrooms and living room were always shut in the winter.

Bountiest Backyards

My guess is that the houses were approximately 30 feet square, so their size would be 900 or so square feet— pretty small, especially given that most families out there had plenty of kids—probably an average of five or six. That's why her dad added those two rooms.

But the spacious backyards were large and useful. Remember, the lots were generous, even after some were cut in two to make Angelo Street. My guess is that Rudy's lot was just shy of three-quarters of an acre. Here is the list of things grown in the Rodolfi backyard, off the top of Rudy's head, when I asked her the question, "Tell me about your backyard":

We had two cows, two hogs, chickens, rabbits, ducks, turkeys, grapes galore, all kinds of vegetables—corn, carrots, tomatoes, beans, peas, lettuce, cabbage, radishes. . . Oh, and fruit trees with apples, pears, plums, cherry. . . and berries like goose, currants and black berries.

I asked her to help me draw their backyard. I've included it in the Appendix. Her father built a small barn for the cows, a hog house for the pigs, an enclosure for the rabbits, one for the chickens and baby chicks, and the obligatory well and outhouse. After he rested for a bit, he added a garage next to the menagerie and garden.

The Rodolfis eventually purchased a lot down the street, just south of the Dellamartes, for more garden space. It was on a hill that ran down into a creek that fed into the ravine. They planted more grapevines there as well as sweet potatoes, green peppers, tomatoes, squash and pumpkins. It was the mrs' job to prepare, plant, harvest, and preserve all the fruit and vegetables the family did not consume during the summer and fall. Rudy created a mental view of that lot for me:

The creek ran east and west on that lot. There were tons of willow trees growing on its banks. Dad would cut those little willow saplings and I would take them and use them to tie the grape vines to the strings or wires.

Except for staples such as flour, sugar and condiments, the Rodolfis were fairly self-sufficient, as were most of the villagers. Such skill and craftmanship for the husbandry and cooking came from the Old Country, and neighbors were happy to share, coordinate and cooperate with each other, such as in butchering hogs, which I will discuss in Chapter Six.

I asked Rudy what they did with the garbage they accumulated. "Most of everything left over was fed to the animals. There was a junkman who came around once a month to remove anything we couldn't haul away ourselves. But that wasn't much."

Talking about her dad tending the ranchette of a backyard, she offered a description of what he wore doing chore work and for other activities:

Dad was pretty typical in the wardrobe department. Like most miners he had three outfits: work, casual and dress. As a miner he wore bib overalls, denim shirt, and work shoes. At home he changed to clean bibs, blue shirt and his Romeo shoes (i.e., slip-ons with elastic sides) over clean white socks. In the garden he put on work shoes again. For weddings and funerals he had one blue suit, a dark blue tie, and ankle-high black leather shoes. His ever-present corncob pipe was stuck between his teeth.

Pryor School was on the northern frontier of Springfield when it was established in 1913. Created at the behest of officials from Jones & Adams Coal Co., who wanted a school in the area for the children of coal miners, it was one of the smallest in Springfield Township and the furthest from downtown. It even had a rural route mailing address. In May 1936 when students were busy playing baseball on the field (and watching a photographer), its future looked secure. That year the school board voted to build a new but small, modern building at a cost of $15,000. It would be renamed after John H. Piper who donated the ground for the building at the corner of Vincent Street and Piper Road in Devereux Heights. The portable and temporary buildings that had served until then would be demolished.

The picture changed in the early 1970s, however, when its usefulness was questioned. After the district announced it was considering closing it, the north side community expressed angry opposition. "We're not asking for anything except to be left alone with our own neighborhood schools," one woman told the school board. Closing it would save $10,000 a year, the board said. Piper School's enrollment was down to just 50 students and it didn't help that it had been put on probation by the state for having three grades in each of its two classrooms. The school was closed after the 1974 school year. FILE/THE STATE JOURNAL-REGISTER

Pryor School's two temporary buildings on the left and (my guess) the new Piper School is being constructed on the right. (Courtesy SJ-R, May 7, 2016)

Chapter Four

The Village School

A community is not of much value without certain elements. You need infrastructure, such as roads and bridges. You need stores, such as a grocery and/or a general store. You need either a doctor or other medical provider, or close access to one. You need a place of worship or close access to one. And, like it or not, you need a tavern. But one other indispensable requirement is a school for the youngins.

Remember in the last chapter when Devereux Heights was just getting started as a community? People began purchasing lots soon after the new village was platted in 1913. These new people had children, so a school was the next step. The poor miners had no wherewithal or time to organize, fund and build a school, so the city of Springfield's School Board stepped in. Why didn't Mr. Devereux and his coal company provide for one, since their new mine created the need?

Part of the reason may have been that Jones & Adams Mine, just a mile southeast of the new addition of Devereux Heights, was coincidentally planning to open a school on or near its property that same year. My guess is that Jones & Adams needed to support its miners with a school for their children, and it realized the Chicago-Springfield Mine's employees needed one as well. They figured it was the neighborly thing to do.

In a scathing editorial about the deplorable "settlement of foreigners" in the November 7, 1917 edition of the *Illinois State Register*, the writer provides us, in addition to the condemnation of the "un-American" settlers, with insight how the area's first school was started:

For years the children had to cross "Deadman's Crossing" – a very dangerous railroad crossing, to get to the Ridgely School, some distance away. Recently, however, the board of education built a school house for the little settlement and called it "Pryor school." There are three rooms in the school house. The children are Italian, Lithuanian, Slavok[sic], Russian Jews and Polish.

In a September 3, 1913 newspaper article detailing the Springfield School Board's August minutes, it explains how the school got its name:

The school located at the Jones & Adams coal mine, northeast of the city, was named the Pryor school, in appreciation of the efforts of Superintendent [John W.] Pryor of the mine to have it located there.

Growing Pains

The children from Devereux (some of whom had gone to Ridgely the previous year) were excited to begin going to their own school in August, 1913, for the 1913-1914 school year. The school was apparently a makeshift structure based on another newspaper account calling it "a portable building." In the middle of that first school year, when the children had just returned to school after Christmas vacation, there was already trouble with the same building.

Question was raised [in a Springfield School Board Meeting] as to the method to pursue in the case of the Pryor school, which building is in bad shape and as a result of improper heating facilities in which, school was dismissed at noon yesterday. By the terms of the contract involved, it is incumbent upon the Jones & Adams Coal company to keep the building in repair. . . "

I'm sure Mine Superintendent Pryor made sure the little school named after him was repaired immediately. However, within three years, another, bigger, problem raised its head: overcrowding. This one was vexing to Superintendent Pryor, the community and the school board. According to an article in the *Register* dated September 2, 1917, there was a contingent of 100 children at Pryor, which the tiny school could not accommodate.

How'd they grow so many kids so fast, is the question? Well, assuming each family had four children of school age, there would have to be at least 25 families in the "school district" area. And, of course, there were some young couples who didn't have children yet. So there must have been 40 or more families in homes in and around Devereux.

In those days people did have several children in each family. My dad grew up just south of Reservoir Park, that 24 acres of several city blocks that now contains Lanphier High School, Memorial Stadium and Robin Roberts Ball Park. His neighborhood was called "Rabbit Row" because people there had so many kids. One family had 21, but the average was more like seven to ten. So it does make sense that there were 100 school-aged kids roaming around Deveraux.

There are two or three more factors for that explosive growth. First, the mining company immediately built ten four-room houses for miners and employees with families. Those would have housed ten families right off the bat. Second, miners likely began buying up those desirable acre lots almost from the get-go. And third, there were surely some families who lived or rented houses around the little burg. Oh, and don't forget about the men who worked for "the zinc works," that smelter across the tracks. They lived in company housing and would have had a significant number of children. And, as mentioned previously, the school needed to serve two mining communities, just a mile or so apart.

Pupils Placed in Limbo

Back to the problem with Devereux's 100 kids having no school alternative. That newspaper article referred to was entitled PUPILS REJECTED BY TWO SCHOOLS. There was a brouhaha brought about in the community of Devereux when it petitioned to have its children transferred to either or both Sandhill Elementary and Ridgely Elementary.

The newspaper article does not explain the other reason why Devereux's 100 children could not continue attending their own Pryor School: its dilapidated condition. It was never intended to be a permanent structure in the first place. Perhaps the school needed help for that current school year (1917-1918) to put the school back into serviceable condition.

The new village therefore petitioned the two nearest school districts for help. Both Sandhill and Ridgely declined, pointing out that the other was responsible for taking in the children. Finger pointing, naturally.

Most of the children (from both mines) were of Italian descent, so reading between the lines, it sounds to me like there was discrimination involved. The community probably thought so too, which may be why it turned to the Italian Consular agent, a Mr. Picco, for assistance.

The Sangamon County Superintendent of Schools, a Mr. Pruitt, intervened with the suggestion that the children belonged to the closer Sandhill District.

Sandhill had a reasonable argument against accepting more students. They had just built a new facility which had 92 students of their own in the two rooms. Pruitt countered that the "orphaned" students could be accommodated in the old Sandhill school (just vacated), with minimum repairs.

Attendance Problems

This would be a good place to talk about the 600-pound gorilla in the room in those days: school attendance. Illinois was the first state in the country to establish limits on children's hourly and weekly work. This law, passed in 1903, also required that schools keep track of student attendance, to ensure that employers were in compliance of the underlying law. Still, not all children attended school all the time.

This was brought to my attention when Gladys Sefick related what her mother-in-law, Helen "H" (Galassi) Sefick told her:

Helen was the oldest daughter in her family of 12, and she didn't regularly attend school. Her mother always had a lot for her to do at home. And the school was a long walk from their house, Helen explained to me. She wasn't the only girl whose parents kept her home some of the time. It wasn't uncommon, especially for girls, she told me.

As years passed, attendance improved and the school board kept a tighter rein on the importance of mandatory attendance.

School Board Solutions

The next newspaper article I found relating to this issue was published on July 14, 1918, when the 1917-1918 school year just concluded a month previously. The school board's solution was reasonable: "Two buildings of the Pryor school are to be moved to Piper's Addition [just south of Devereux Heights] in order to accommodate the pupils in that neighborhood." It seems that the original site for the "Miners' School," as it was also referred to at the time, was, in fact, very close to the Jones-Adams Mine.

The "new school" would accommodate the six upper grades and leave the first two grades at the former site. The new facilities were placed on Piper Road, at the corner lot of Vincent Street. The rented location soon was purchased when the district put it up for a vote. So the overcrowding situation was alleviated with this temporary, two-school accommodation.

According to a newspaper article dated September 9, 1919, the two-Pryor schools concept became one school again the following school year when the school board voted to close down Pryor School No. 1 because only five pupils enrolled. That was the school close to the Jones-Adams Mine where classes for the first and second grades were conducted. So, Pryor School No. 2, closer to Devereux, now housed all classes, one through eight.

Finally, Some Levity

The first of December, in the middle of the 1918-1919 school year, the serious matters of the school board were greeted with some semblance of humor. Finally, something to laugh about. The paper wrote on that date the following:

Tragedy and comedy chase each other in the coal situation. There is a touch of grim humor in the report that came from the Pryor school this morning that between Friday night and Sunday morning somebody had looted the coal bin of its entire contents. The humor of the situation lies in the fact that the Pryor school is a special institution maintained in the mining settlement of Devereux Heights for the benefit of the children of coal miners.

The Superintendent of Schools, J.M. Allen, decided to close the school for the next full week, which is the time period the coal would have warmed the school house. "There will be no further sessions until the strike breaks or somebody brings back the coal," he announced. The school house had three rooms and about 100 pupils, all of whom were children of coal miners. My guess is that he used the word "strike" in the formal sense that there was a coal strike by the area miners at the time as opposed in a humorous sense.

Student Life

What was Pryor School like in its early years? I am going to pull out several strands of opinion to answer that question from that editorial piece in the November 7, 1917 paper referred before. The title of the Letter to the Editor reads, "Small Settlement Knows Nothing of Outside Affairs." So, that is a hint that the critic is extremely biased about immigrants generally and Devereux's in particular. Still, these snippets will give insight into one perspective about the elementary school, its pupils and parents.

. . . *In the first grade there is this beautiful little Italian girl, who is really under school age, who can sing*

English songs, taught her by the teacher, but who is unable to speak a word of the language. Her musical instinct ability could conquer the difficulties of the language, but without the stimulus of a tune she finds it impossible, or very difficult at least, to talk in a foreign tongue, as English is to her. . .

. . . Pryor School is reached by the Peoria Interurban. Last year one of the teachers froze her hands twice while waiting for the car to bring her back to town. . .

. . . Last year Mrs. S. J. Hanes was instrumental in getting Pryor school an old organ, and when she next visited the school house she found that the mothers of the children, and the children themselves, had decorated that organ with vases of flowers, and bits of embroidery, and fragments of pictures, in an effort to make it look like a Catholic altar. . .

. . . Mrs. S. J. Hanes, of the School Council, is endeavoring to secure a phonograph for use in the school, which is to form the main attraction in the neighborhood. She feels that something is needed to draw the mothers together, and that working from the school house as a social center, civilized ideas of living may be spread among the people.

One Student's School House Memories

Here is another snippet from a student himself about Pryor. It is how Merino Giacomini remembered its tragic end, from his autobiography:

I started elementary school in September, 1930 at what was then known as Pryor School. The building *was an old wooden structure that was completely destroyed in 1934 by a strong windstorm. It was my good fortune that the storm happened late in the evening, or I might not be around today writing this life story. I report this because on the next day, as I viewed the damage, I noticed that a jagged end of one of the roof rafters was driven completely through my desk. [I believe the actual date of the storm was 1936.]*

After much haggling with the school board, the old school was replaced by a new two-story brick building and renamed Piper School. The new school consisted of two large classrooms upstairs. One room for the first through fourth grades and the other for the fifth through eighth grades. The first floor contained a playroom for rainy days, a furnace room and restrooms. The entire staff consisted of two teachers [Mrs. Mueller and Mrs. Weber] *and a woman janitor* [Josie Giacomini; and later, Stella Moore joined her]. *How's that for a small budget?*

According to an article in the local paper, the first principal of Pryor School was Nellie Tomer (1913-1914). Others included Jennie McGlassen (1914-1916), F. H. Rhea (1916-1923), and Florence H. Robertson (1923- 1936).

Piper School

Located about half way up Piper Road, Pryor School served the community longer than I would have thought its useful life would have allowed. But in 1936, the school house yielded, not to a faulty boiler or a weak wall brace, but to a severe wind storm, which Merino alluded to above, that made it uninhabitable.

The community didn't waste any time rebuilding. In fact, my thinking is that it had been underway when the storm hit the old school. That may be why there was no interruption of school that fall. (Notice the picture of both schools in the picture at the beginning of this chapter.) The school name was changed to Piper Elementary School, after John H. Piper who donated the land. It served kindergarten through fifth grades. It was a sturdy, two-story brick building, with the first floor serving as a playroom, kitchenette, and restrooms. The second floor housed two classrooms. It was situated just in front of the original school, and tucked in the southwest corner of Piper Road and Vincent Street. It had a generous school playground with swings and monkey bars, an ample green space plus a baseball field, all enclosed with a fence. Around the school itself was a gravel parking lot. The school complex was 300 feet by 202.5 feet, or about 1.4 acres.

School principals included Florence H. Robertson (1936-1942), Richard P. Stone (1946-1954), and J.E. Bohn, who also served as unofficial superintendent of school, until his full time assignment as superintendent in 1957. (As late as 1960 Bohn was serving the dual role as principal of Bunn School and Piper School.)

"Education Is Fun In Tiny School"

I was delighted to read the article appearing in the *Illinois State Journal* (dated September 22, 1960) with the same title as the heading of this section. Caryl Carstens, the reporter, tells about how special small schools can be. Although by the sixties the one-room country schoolhouse had gone by way of the operator-assisted phone line, Devereux's Piper School retained some of the valuables of school days gone by. Carstens' article is the exact opposite to the above perspective from that woman's negative and discriminatory Letter to the Editor, above.

For example, in Mrs. (Ava) Weber's room, the 23 pupils represented fourth, fifth and sixth grades. (The article uses these grades, instead of the traditional split of 1—4 and 5—8. Maybe they changed somewhere along the line.) She had been at Piper since 1939 and declared "I wouldn't accept another position." The other room was taught by Mrs. Dorothy Greicius at the time. She handled the first three grades, which had a combined 29 pupils.

Sometimes, when practical, the two teachers combined their classes when instructing their students, depending on the subject they were studying. For example, health and social studies may have been handled together.

Carstens points out that "Sometimes the teachers are able to give almost individual instructions because of the smallness of the classes . . . The children are given the same instructions in art, music and physical education that other pupils in the system and have special teachers visiting the school once or twice a week. The speech correctionist also works with those children who need attention."

The two seasoned teachers must have done something right because "[their children's] records compare well with those of students from the other schools . . . when they moved into junior and senior high schools."

The statement of Mrs. Weber's I really enjoyed was about the ease she employed in handling her students which didn't hurt their development in the least. She said, "I personally don't believe in setting down a lot of rules . . . I'm training them for democracy." As a certified teacher who mainly subs, I have the same philosophy and get more out of my charges with the light touch and a sense of humor.

Great Memories of Piper School

Here is a perspective from Laura Galassi's fun memories of Piper Elementary in the late 1950s:

Of course, there was a Fall Festival with homemade baked goods, contests at Halloween for ugliest, funniest, etc. customs. We'd go through the neighborhood selling tickets for it. At Christmas we always had a program with singing, a play, and a musical. In the spring our teacher from the "big room"—grades 4-8—would ump' at our baseball games at recess.

The Fate of Piper School

Piper School was closed for good in 1975. There were two basic reasons for the closure. First, according to a June 18, 1975 article in the paper, "The state evaluators didn't like the practice of putting more than one grade in a room, as was necessary at Piper. Three grades were in each of the two rooms. . . [Second,] The school administration also wants to save some money . . . [in the education fund]."

The remedy was transporting the 48 remaining students, with ample money from the transportation fund, to nearby Sandhill Elementary just northwest of Devereux a mile or so.

However, not everyone was pleased with the idea. The article explains that a parents group said that the parents as a whole strongly opposed the closing of the school. "The neighborhood is growing. We want to maintain the school and expand it." The community also didn't like the idea of busing its children to Sandhill. The last rationale was that "the land was donated specifically for use as a school and couldn't be used for other purposes or sold by the board." In the end, the Springfield School District 186

Board voted to close the school at its June 1974 meeting. (District 186 was in charge of both Piper and Sandhill since the city had annexed Devereux in 1967.)

The citizens of Devereux did not take the closing lying down. They regrouped and continued their battle with the School Board. The following year the parents' group again petitioned the Board to reopen Piper School, backed up by about 700 signatures in favor of the reopening. The Board, however, was not persuaded and denied the petition.

I imagine quite a few parents seething from the closure sent their children to St. Aloysius Grade School, if they were Catholic—maybe even if they weren't. Piper School was eventually torn down and replaced by modern houses. No one would guess there was ever a school there.

Sandhill Neighborhood

Since this chapter has discussed Sandhill Elementary School and its relationship, at times, with Devereux schools, I will use this section to mention a little more about the neighborhood of Sandhill.

Sandhill is very close in proximity to Devereux. It is more a region than a distinct area with boundaries. It lies just north of Devereux and then both west and east, along Sandhill Road. It is bisected by Peoria Road which continues north across the Sangamon River.

The region west of Peoria Road I'll call West Sandhill. In the old days, I suppose it contained around 50 families, maybe fewer. That is where the elementary school was located. Several small roads branch off of Sandhill Road. There is still a small community there, including a mobile home court. On the east side of the river ("East Sandhill"), Sandhill Road runs due east for a half a mile and then turns suddenly south into Shaler Road, which meets Bissel Road in another half mile. Three tributary roads come off of this E. Sandhill Road: Bachman, Riverside Drive and Piper Lane. There were probably another 50 families that lived in this region on the east side of the river, back-when.

Devereux resident Donna Holliday remembers school bus drivers referring to Devereux as well as high school students north of the village as "those Sandhill kids."

Jim Galassi summed up the relationship by saying, "We in Devereux thought of all the areas around us as one region, you might say: those across the tracks, west of us,

as well as those across the Bypass, north of us."

Josephine "Josie" Giacomini (center) was Piper School's first custodian ("caretaker"). This picture recognizes her 25 years of service. (Courtesy Nancy Bartlett)

The Jailhouse Tavern and Fofi's Market. If there is one iconic place that defines Devereux it is this combined structure. The present owner is currently revamping the old building, which is good for her and the village.

Chapter Five

Town Commerce

I **had to dig pretty deep to come up with very many** **local businesses in Devereux.** For some years the village's citizens had to trek into Springfield for the necessities of life. But as time went on, enterprising people "saw a need and filled it," as the entrepreneurial spirit moved them.

The following are some businesses that most of the people I interviewed remembered, either themselves or through their parents or grandparents. Where I can, I mention the time frame, since some were begun early on in the 19-teen years and others didn't get started until the '40s and '50s.

Jailhouse Tavern

If there is a trademark for Devereux Heights, it is the Jailhouse Tavern. It sits on the northwest corner of Mayden Avenue and Donna Street. Whenever the village's name is invoked in and around Springfield, people may not know much about it, but many people have heard about the iconic Jailhouse Tavern. Local legend has it that the building was in fact a holding jail in the old days. In addition to the catchy name, there are actual steel bars on the windows to add credibility to the claim.

Al Kenal told me he knows the real story behind the tavern and its name:

My dad, George Kenal, wanted to start a tavern and talked to the Fofis about renting the store next to their grocery store. They agreed, so Dad had to next get a license at the County Building. The clerk asked him what the name of his new business was going to be. Dad said he never thought of it, so the clerk asked him, "What's it look like on the outside?" Dad said it was just a normal building but had bars on the three front windows, kind of like a jail. The clerk then suggested, "Why don't you call it the Jailhouse Tavern?" Dad thought that was as good a name as any and that's how it came about.

Dad was a miner working the mine at Cantrall. So, Mom [Mary (Galassi) Kenal] ran the tavern during the day and Dad would come in at night to relieve her. They eventually sold the business, and it has had a bunch of owners since.

You will read in the rest of this book memory excerpts from locals alluding to this favorite watering hole. I asked Jim Bartlett, who at 87 has lived in Devereux his entire life, if he had any pictures of the Jailhouse. The laid-back Jim perked up immediately in his easy chair and chimed in, "You don't need an old picture of it; it looks the same today as it did when I was a boy." He should know because he grew up just across the street from it.

He and his wife Nancy Willis still live near it—just four houses north on the east side of Donna Street. Nancy worked there for four years as a waitress in her younger days and said it holds about 30 thirsty customers. She told me lots of politicians would frequent the little tavern.

Ninety-one-year-old Rudy Rodolfi, whom I interviewed at her East Peoria cabin (which lies about as close to the Illinois River as a house can) told me the Jail-house (and the grocery next to it) was originally owned by Pasquale and Maria Fofi. They had three children, Erman, Guareno, and Eva. She confirmed that the tavern business (not the property it is on) has had many owners over the years. Eva, who married Tony Antonacci, worked at both places—her folks' grocery store and the bar. Nancy added that whenever the tavern had turtle on the menu, it sold out fast. She also said the spaghetti was to die for.

About the days in the late '30s when his dad ran it, Al recently told me more:

Dad was in the mines all day so Mom ran it. She opened it at 10:00 in the morning. When he came home, she would leave. Dad would run it until 10:30 at night. If the guys were still playing "Pitch" or "Rum," he would walk out and tell them to "Lock the door when you leave."

Brad Mills came up with what he thinks may be the complete owners' list of the tavern business. He's not sure of the exact order, but here's what he thinks it may be: the Fofi parents, Erm and Eva Fofi; George Kenal, Curley and Marge Jones; Tom Stevens; Curley and Marge again; a group with the Earls; Nick Murphy; the Earls alone; Bob Springfloat; Bill and Sis Hufker; and for the past 15 years Pam Meyers-Jerome, under the longest-running ownership.

Pam recently told me, while I was visiting with her in her tavern, that she bought the place from Rene Miller who had it for five years, and before her Mickey Greenslate.

When she purchased it in 2004, Pam had renovated the bar area with brand-new hardwood custom-made furniture. The bar back and bar top are sure good-looking and add class to the place. She runs a good business: you can tell that the minute you walk in. It has several tables, a pool table, ATM machine, modern jukebox, and a row of those obligatory gambling machines.

Brad, like so many others, worked at the tavern. At fifteen, it was his first job and he sometimes would act as cook although his main job was in the kitchen and on the tables. He eventually took on the job as bartender when there was a need, even before he was of age.

Back when I was growing up [Brad explained], they served food on Friday and Saturday nights, plus noons during the week. Turtle was a special treat because they are hard to get. There was one guy, Paul Austin, who was quite the hunter and trapper, who also had the knack of catching turtles. He would take a stick and somehow find them at the water's edge by tapping down in the mud.

Both Bartletts told me that there used to be neighborhood parties down at the Jailhouse Tavern. "They were big affairs, with fried fish, burgoo, and a band playing one or two times a year." When I asked Jim where they fished around there, he said some guys fished at the river but there was some big pond around there where they got most of the fish. He couldn't recall where exactly the pond was.

If you want to experience Devereux's past today, you can still walk in Pam's Jailhouse and have a cold one. I did that and thought, as I looked around, "If only walls could talk."

Fofi's Market

The other memorialized business in Devereux Heights was Fofi's Market, the two-story brick building hugging the Jailhouse (via a small garage) and situated right on the corner. It's now apartments and looks to me a little worn out. It is actually undergoing renovation under the capable care of Pam Meyers-Jerome.

Like so many other high school-aged kids, Rudy worked there after school. "I earned 50 cents a week and gave half of it to my mom, who used it to buy their first kitchen table and chairs set from the Sukalaski's, another Devereux family."

As soon as you walk in [Rudy, describing the store],
you see the counter on the left wall. It had candy on it. It
also had a metal rack that held the records of everyone's
running accounts until payday, on Friday nights. Toward the
back on that side was a door to the outside. In the back of
the store was the meat counter (with fresh meats). Behind
the white display case was a big wooden walk-in freezer.
The east wall had shelves with all dry goods and canned
foods. The middle aisle was filled with large wooden bins,
containing fresh fruit, flour, sugar, potatoes, etc.

Pasquale Fofi was a coal miner who apparently
saved his money because he purchased that corner lot in
1918, in his wife's name, and built the brick building within
the next couple of years. He left coal mining in 1922 and
opened Fofi's Market in early 1923.

Al Kenal recalls the building ownership issue a little
differently when he told me:

As I recall, the first owner of those buildings were
Ray and Margret Dively. There were actually three buildings
there at first: the one on the west, then one in the middle,
and then the brick, two-story one on the corner. The middle
one looked like a small garage and was later made part of

the west one for the tavern. The Divelys ran the grocery store first and later sold it all to the Fofis.

What is clear is that Mrs. (August) Fofi bought Lot 47 (on which the building rests) in 1918, according to records. My reconstruction of the events is that the Fofis built the building and operated the market for many years and around 1940 rented it to the Divelys for perhaps five years. Then they took it over again, this time with Eva and Erm running it until 1963 when they called it quits and retired for good. The two children also operated the Jailhouse Tavern for a few years as we saw in the previous section.

I am still curious about when the other two structures were built that attach to Fofi's Market. My guess is that Pasquale Fofi built a garage for a truck to deliver groceries and meat to area customers, then he built another small structure attached to the garage for storage. Finally, he added on to that west building to the north as his grocery store business grew. That west building was either unnecessary when George Kenal wanted to use it as a tavern or Pasquale felt the rent from it was worth losing the space.

I believe that Mr. Fofi and his wife, then their children, ran the grocery store continuously for 40 years, (except for those five years they rented it to the Divelys) until 1963 when Donna and Laura Galassi, who used to go in there all the time, told me it closed. (Someone else confirmed that that year it closed.) They were in high school at the time (when I was in the class between them).

The Fofis likely resided in the upstairs apartment until they could afford a house of their own, which they built on one lot west, just beyond the stores, with their children. Eva, the Fofi daughter, her own daughter plus her husband, Tony Antonacci, then lived upstairs in the apartment over the market. When her parents passed on, Eva and Tony had the Fofi house moved onto the lot behind the stores, on Donna Street, and lived there the rest of their lives.

The brother and sister team efficiently ran the grocery store. Erm's domain was his butcher shop in the back of the store, while Eva took care of the groceries part. Erm first cut his teeth in the grocery business by apprenticing at the Italian-American Import Store in Springfield. (As a child, I took many a trip there with my

Italian mother. It was run by the Frascos—Mary and her brother "Frenchie.") Nancy Bartlett continued the Fofi story: "When Eva and Tony died, their three children sold the house to Tom Meitz who still lives there."

Nancy ranted and raved about Erm's Italian sausage. "Everybody loved it. It was simple enough, just pork, garlic and salt and pepper. But, boy, was it delicious!"

Mary (Soltys) Yoggerst described Fofi's credit system. Regular customers—which was most of the town— would purchase items "on time" with Eva writing down their purchases and allowing the customers to settle up at the end of the month. (Mom did that when she shopped at Kohlrus' in our neighborhood on Converse Avenue.) It was a common method of paying for groceries in the old days since money was tight and there was little or no bank credit.

Devereux's First Grocery Store

This is the grocery store nobody had ever heard of, until librarian-local historian Curtis Mann unearthed it for me. Nobody alive today knows that a man named Jacob Kauth has the distinction of being the village's first grocer, just three years after the settlement began selling lots. Kauth purchased lot 55 in Devereux in early September

1915. That is the corner lot at Interurban Avenue and South Street, now Mayden Avenue. It is not too far a leap to conclude he built his grocery store right after the land purchase. The first record of his being in that business is a reference as "grocer and meat market owner" in a May 20, 1916 *Illinois State Register* article about possible annexation.

Kauth likely lived "across the tracks" in the area called "Smelterville," in one of the Zinc Works company housing or near it, other library records imply. One can also assume his neighbors in that area patronized his grocery store, as well as Devereuxites.

Three years later he was again referred to in the newspaper, this time in connection with a holdup at his butcher shop "near the Devereux Mine." The long article about that and several other related armed robberies around Springfield mentions Kauth's wife and another employee, a butcher named "Adam," as the only ones in the store at the time. Kauth himself was nearby in his barn. The three gunmen made off with a tin can containing $880.

Jacob Kauth apparently had an unsavory side to him too, with several recorded brushes with the law. In 1915 he pleaded guilty and fined $20 for "selling liquor in anti-saloon territory." He was again charged with the same offense and placed bond in 1918. Five years later (on September 20, 1923), he again was in trouble, this time for a charge of "padding pauper claims," for which he was indicted.

[Note: To explain the last paragraph better, it appears that a new law was created in 1907 that allowed townships to vote to be wet or dry. Springfield Township (in which Devereux used to be) voted to become dry in the April 1908 election. This meant that Devereux would have to be dry when it was created. I am not sure if Devereux ever was wet before the end of prohibition. This pertained to selling alcohol in establishments.]

Apparently, Kauth indeed became a pauper himself six years later (April 13, 1929) when he filed a voluntary petition for bankruptcy, listing his debts as $6,014 against assets of only $2,974.

It seems likely that the Kauth Grocery and Meat Market and the Fofi's Market did not overlap—thus did not compete—since the former probably went out of business (due to the above legal troubles) right when the latter was starting his business.

Mayden's Country House

The only true restaurant in the village was called Mayden's Country House, a large white residence on Mayden Avenue, south and east a few blocks from Fofi's on the south side of the road. An imposing house on a hill, it was owned by Frank and Teresa Mayden. Teresa had inherited it from her parents. The restaurant itself was a later addition to Devereux, having been established in the late '30s or early '40s. The dining room was an obvious rectangle addition facing the road, with the commercial kitchen under it in the basement. Jim Bartlett worked there when just a youngster about 12-years old, which would have been around 1944.

The house is much older and had been part of the small Mayden farm where hogs were raised for several years. It must have been ten or more acres because it extended from east of the house all the way down the street west to Piper Road and then south as far as Willow Lane (and maybe farther), most of it enclosed with a wire fence. That west end of the farm was unimproved with lots of trees and brush plus a frog pond.

The interior of the house was fancy, "very beautiful on the inside," commented Nancy Bartlett. "When you walked in the dining room, you saw all these antiques all over the walls." The food was served buffet style, a novelty around the area at the time, someone mused.

Brad Mills, who grew up in Devereux on Piper Road, where he still lives, told me the residence used to be called "The Mayden Mansion" by locals because of the impressive image it portrayed. The Maydens lived there in the residence part even while they ran the business. He heard that when it became a restaurant it catered to not only the locals but also politicians, other dignitaries, and some shady characters from Chicago. (Al Capone's name was offered up but that is pure rumor, as it always is .) The events put on there at the restaurant was the closest thing to Devereux high society as there was in the unassuming village.

The Maydens closed the restaurant in the '60s. Somebody told me the specific reason for closing was that the water line in front of the place broke and prevented easy access for quite some time. Regardless if that was true or not, the Maydens weren't earning a lot of money off of the business and apparently didn't have family money to fall back on. Frank had also worked all those years at the nearby slaughterhouse (on Stockyard Road) to supplement their income and, after the closing, Teresa cooked at Clayville, near Pleasant Plains, for many years.

"The Mayden Mansion" still stands there, painted in its trademark color, although with new residential owners and up-to-date renovations. As I stopped by the side of the road to take a picture of it, I had the feeling it was looking back at me, still with a sense of pride for its illustrious past. I smiled back at it, waved out of respect, and drove on.

Bootlegging

What? You don't think this was a business? Tell that to all the impoverished families in Devereux (and elsewhere) who lived on a hand-to-mouth existence during those "Roaring Twenties."

And, a big business at that. Even though it only lasted a decade or so, it helped the economy of the "little village that could". When the word bootlegging came up in conversations, Devereux Heights would also come up. It was a major industry, albeit illegal, for more than a few resourceful opportunists. Jim and Nancy Bartlett set the stage for this topic with an example from the Galassis:

Assunta had bootlegging money in her family. The men only cooked and drove—no violent activities.

The year 1920 brought with it the passage of the 18th Amendment, which banned the manufacture, transportation, importation, and sale of intoxicating liquors in the United States. It also caused more than a little consternation in the mostly Italian communities across the country. What were they to do about their wine? Many Italian homes already contained barrels of fermenting wines in basements. (My sister and I would run around the two big barrels in our Grandfather Roscetti's basement and thought it a normal part of any Italian basement.)

Everybody from the North End I talked to about the old days in Devereux would eventually suggest, "Don't forget to tell about all the bootlegging going on during Prohibition." [I was perplexed that hardly any other Springfieldian ever heard about this community, let alone its reputation as a major bootlegging locus.] So, in addition to making wine for their own family consumption, many resourceful and needy Devereuxites ignited their latent commercial aptitudes and had at it, switching mostly to brewing spirits rich alcohol.

One incident that comes up with locals in connection with this subject is the shooting that took place on the porch of the Dellamarte house on Angelo Street. Here is Jim Bartlett's take on it:

Sesto [Paoni], who was Nancy's uncle and a man he was in cahoots with, sold some of the whiskey and kept the money. When the Chicago guys came down to Devereux to pick up the supply, they knew it had been tampered with.

The way it ended was Sesto's partner was shot and they came after Sesto, who ran all the way to the end of Interurban when they caught up to him. They beat him up bad, but he snuck away across the tracks.

I later asked Charlie Bedolli if the man died. He offered up his best toothy smile and said, "Don't the Mafia usually make sure the guy's dead before they leave?" It was quickly covered up, as too much publicity would put a damper on the Chicago—Devereux—St. Louis booze trade triangle. Sesto, who had worked in the mines, thought it prudent to get the hell out of Devereux as fast as he could.

He returned to his wife and kids from Washington state (or other points northwest, rumor had it) after four years of letting things cool off.

Al Kenal told me that his father, who was a bachelor in his young 20s at the time, earned $100 a week from cooking mash. That was a boat load of money back then. "And he didn't have to worry about the law—that was taken care of." Lots of other coal miners were doing the same business with the same impunity.

Nancy Bartlett added to the stories about those days:

Over at Domenic Giacomini's house, which we had later lived in, the basement windows all had bars on them. In my sister's and my bedroom was a trapdoor in our closet leading to the coal bin, for a fast getaway, I suppose.

After a little more prodding, Nancy thought of another episode:

Nobody had good jobs in those days, so everybody was in the whiskey business, even Jim's grandfather. Paonis in the big house on Mayden had a half basement dug out just for the business. "Chicago" would come over and pick up their booze. It was in 10-gallon cans. They would come to town with a semi and pick it all up. It was something to see.

Here is a reference to bootlegging and wine in my mother's biography, under the heading, "Making Vino":

Grandpa and most Italian families in Springfield, if not the country, made their own wine. During the Prohibition period, from 1919 through 1932, he continued to produce enough wine for his family and a few friends and relatives. Mom emphasized that, "Papa never sold any wine, ever. That just wasn't him. Mr. Cardoni ran a [bootleg] place in Devereaux [Heights], but not Papa."

During the anti-alcohol era, Grandpa did try his hand at making beer in his basement for himself and with some success. He almost got in trouble for doing so from an unlikely source. There was a bootlegger down the street across from my childhood home [on Converse Avenue, just west of 19th Street]. Mom said the man lived in an old two-story gambrel roof farmhouse and his name was Mr. Gragetski.[5] In order to keep the heat off of him, he would use other peoples' names as purchasers of large volumes of yeast and sugar, critical ingredients in beer. One such name he used was Bert Roscetti—not a nice thing to do to a neighbor. When the federal agents inspected the grocer's records and discovered Grandpa's name, they paid him a visit.

He was of course shocked at the accusation and calmly invited the agents to take a look at his distillery in the basement. When they saw his two barrels of wine and about the same quantity of beer, they were convinced he was not selling his brew. They apologized and left him to his small just-for-home operation.

Alex Talmant [a neighbor across the street from the Roscetti's who later became a general in the Air Force] recalls Grandpa's wine making:

My exposure to 'Ole' Bert consisted mainly of my helping him pick dandelions during those months the coal miners were idle, July through September. My first sample of Bert's product was when I was 7 or 8 years [old]—and my last was when Dorothy and I were married—and came by from the church to get the Roscetti's blessing (1943). [6]

Hugo Antonacci [Mom's first cousin] also mentioned to me that the Italian men used dandelions for making wine. I had never heard of that before.

Since I'm on the subject of booze, I'll mention a not-much-discussed family truth. Grandpa, like too many husbands of his day, would take frustrations out on his wife and hit Grandma. This was not an everyday situation, but it occurred from time to time. It was usually either precipitated by, or in conjunction with, drinking too much.

Rudy told me in her handwritten notes (that she had ready for me when I arrived for our first interview) that "our dad had bootleggers come in our basement. Dad ran a wagonload of sugar late at night. We were not allowed to ever go in our basement." That shows the inherent dangers of working with professional bootleggers. I'm sure there were others in the village willing to expose themselves and their families to great risk for the benefit of earning money during the worst economic calamity in our nation's history. It was peril and opportunity.

"During the Prohibition Years, John 'Miz' Geyston, who lived up there on East Street in the middle house, turned his sugar and cereal into moonshine and sold it to eager buyers," somebody explained to me during our garage conversation.

If you want to be shocked and dismayed at this lovely village, see the article in the Appendix for several stories in the local paper that chronicles more of the sordid side of Devereux during those prohibition days.

Wobble Inn

The Wobble Inn was no inn at all; it was a tavern—one of three in Devereux. My guess is that it was a functioning business in the '30s through the '50s.

Rudy remembers as a child (in the early '30s) that it was owned by Frank Struckel, who lived behind it in a house on the adjoining lot. The entrepreneurial Struckel constructed the two-story building first as income property for two apartments. (Jim Bartlett told me his parents rented one of them while Jim was a child before moving into their home across the street from the Jailhouse Tavern.) Struckel later changed the bottom part into a tavern and had a fellow named Edwards run it. Not much later, he rented it to "Wob" Sefick, who gave it its new name and operated it for several years. (One of my classmates at St.

Al's grade school was John "Fibber" Sefick, who was Wob's nephew.)

The tavern was a large place, with a barroom and also a sizable ballroom. It was situated on the west edge of town, where the two avenues (Interurban and Mayden) met at the northwest corner. Its claim to fame was a selfless one: Nice guy Wob used to show free movies on Saturday night during the summers on the lawn next to his establishment. Lots of older local folks remember those summer Saturday movies as some of their golden moments growing up.

(We had the same open-sky Saturday night shows on the main baseball infield of Fairview Park when I played Little League there in the '50s. The concession stand was right behind the backstop where Mom helped sell popcorn and soda and candies. Good times in those innocent days. A Devereux carpenter by the name of Vic Gent, married to Linda Giacomini, helped Dad, Bill Cellini, Sr., and others build that park.)

As you can tell, practically everyone in Devereux received nicknames early on. Mr. Sefick earned his name because he sort of wobbled when he walked, kind of like a penguin. (Someone told me he had actually acquired that limp from an injury. No matter, a nickname is a nickname in Devereux.)

The Barn Tavern

The third tavern was the Barn Tavern, which was located just a few lots south of Mayden on the east side of West Street. It was built by Ray and Mary Menendez "from brick Poston Brick Yard couldn't sell," their grandson Lou Menendez told me.

The name was taken from the days when the Menendezs raised and fattened hogs there, across the street from their home. Lou told me his grandparents got slop to feed the hogs from restaurant scraps at one of the downtown hotels.

The Menendez family converted the barn into a tavern in the 1940s. It was one large room with a long bar and accommodated around 50 or more customers. For a short time, Lou's Aunt Frances ran a grocery store in a small room on the north side of the building.

When his grandparents passed, their heirs leased the tavern to other operators, including the Knights of Columbus, and then closed it in 1964.

The Roll Inn Tavern & Dancehall

I suppose technically there were really four places to wet your whistle around Devereux if we count the Roll Inn. The reason I don't really think of it as "of" Devereux is because it was located north of the village, close to where old Route 66 Bypass runs into Peoria Road. In fact, the 3.25 acres it occupied lay east of and close to where the tipple of the Devereux Mine was built. Nowadays, there are no remnants of the famous dance hall and bar, but there is some of the Reynolds Auction house still there, along with the Coco's Café, now out of business.

Both, Mary Yoggerst and Nancy Bartlett, went on and on about how great the Roll Inn was. It had, according to Mary, the granddaughter of the owner Felix Golab, "the best dance floor in town."

Everybody in the know told me that place was built by hand with the help of the entire Golab family. It probably took two or three years. The daughters would clean many of the exterior bricks, one after the other, night after night.

The superb dance floor itself was also lovingly put together by the Golab girls—Sophie, Josephine, Mary and Betty.

All that hard work by family members paid off when the Roll Inn opened in 1941 by the family patriarch Felix Golab who was also a coal miner. Later, his sons John and Ed came in as partners. John's wife Viola took it over when her husband passed in 1975. Under the Golabs, the Roll Inn had a remarkable run of 35 years.

Sold at auction in 1977 (due to Viola's declining health), it became Missionarry Mary's under new ownership. That's when it changed from polka to rock music. The building burned to the ground in 1983 in a spectacular fire aided by dried out rafters and flooring.

Rudy told me it was "a *real* Polish polka dancehall." The Golabs were Polish, as were many northenders, so that kind of music was a big hit. (It is one of my favorite types of music. I have no rhythm and can't dance, but I sure put on like I can when "Roll out the barrel . . ." or a similar polka song starts up with that accordion sound. Love it, love it, love it! I'm actually playing it on YouTube as I write these words.)

When you walked in the establishment, there was an air of fun and excitement. You saw the bar in the front on the left side and a kitchen toward the right. From that point you walked into a large dance hall, under an open, wooden arched ceiling, which carried your eye all the way to the back. It had a 40-foot band stage across the back wall, with the dance hall room accommodating 300 happy, perspiring dancers. The family lived upstairs.

In a feature article in the Springfield paper (April 10, 1976), Viola is quoted as saying, "People came from everywhere—Peoria and St. Louis—and they came every week for this polka music. They came even in the summer time, and we don't have any air conditioning. We still get the big crowds."

Quite a few Devereux people were recipients of the Golabs' giving nature too. It was not unusual at all for the Golabs to give needy neighbors food especially in the form of meats. One person backed up this sentiment by telling me "They were all generous. If they knew you needed something, they would help."

Vince Galassi, Inc.

The businessman mentioned most to me as being the most successful Devereux Heights citizen (in the modern era) was Vince Galassi. [Note: This Galassi family is not related at all to the other Galassis I mention in the book.] In today's business parlance, some of these terms might apply to Vince: connector, influencer and entrepreneur. He was a real go-getter, I was repeatedly told, and had his hands in many things. His most recognizable business interest was his car repair garage and salvage yard, which formed the foundation for his overall business holdings.

Down on Piper Road, just south of Mayden, there was situated his one-acre salvage operation, on the east side of the street, hidden down on what is today called Ida Mae Lane. Those wrecked cars were a major source of parts he used to repair cars and trucks at his garage on Peoria Road (where present-day Jungle Jim's Restaurant sits). One of his daughters told me he got his start at a similar shop when he was 16. Once he learned the trade sufficiently, her savvy father decided to go on his own, thinking, "If they can do it, so can I." Vince named his business Central Body and Paint Shop.

When his nephew, "Gus" Morosi, returned from the Army, Vince took him on as his partner. That repair shop turned into a very profitable venture for him for 40 years. From time to time, he was able to obtain city contracts to maintain and repair city vehicles, police cars in particular, thus expanding his business.

With an unpretentious home on Piper Road (across the street from Piper School) where he raised his family, Vince evolved into a real estate investor along the way and made that another profit center. He built and purchased a number of income-producing houses and apartments. For example, he eventually replaced the salvaged yard with several income properties that still lie at the end of the short lane.

People told me he was a shrewd businessman who had a nose for investment opportunities. The word from everybody I asked was that Vince was also very tight with a buck. That's not surprising because that is a trait that is usually the mark of any good businessman. Jim Bartlett told me that "He gave lots of people jobs in those days; he was a good guy, in my opinion." So, during the course of his life, while he acquired financial resources, Vince also gained influence as well as appreciation, especially in the village of Devereux.

Here are his daughters' comments about their parents. Both Donna and Laura met with me over coffee at the local Panera restaurant. (From time to time they would call their older sister, Barbara, on the phone to verify information.) It was nice seeing them again: We attended Lanphier High School together, Donna being one year ahead of me and Laura one year behind me.

Vince Galassi had done well enough to be able to send each of his daughters through college—no small feat in the 1960s. He was thus a "good provider," they said.

"Dad always emphasized the critical importance of an education. He often said, 'That's one thing they can never take away from you.'" All girls were excellent students: Laura has a master's degree and was a teacher, Donna has not one but two doctorate degrees, and Barbara has her bachelor's in education, having taught for 33 years.

Vince was smart too, even though, like many people in those days, he only had an eighth-grade education. He was especially good with numbers.

The other points the girls wanted to make about their dad were these:

Dad was friendly and also thoughtful. . . Mom was always behind the scenes, but she was right up there with him as far as all the business decisions were concerned. . . He was a hard worker, with a strong work ethic, working from 7:00 a.m. until 7:00 p.m. at the garage. . . Mom was the same way as a homemaker. . . Dad was very strict with us. He wouldn't let us date until we were 16. . . He and Mom never drank and would not allow us to go anywhere where there was alcohol. . . He was definitely a mover and a shaker and was active in Republican politics. Nelson Howarth [a two-term mayor of Springfield] was a friend of our family's. . . Dad was most proud of his family, not just his accomplishments . . . He always said, "Your reputation is the most important thing in your life, even over education," meaning your name.

He was an active member, along with friends Ed Best and Noah Neil, in the North-End GOP Improvement

Club and, as such, Laura pointed out to me, "[he] was very busy in working to get the [north-end] area upgraded and developed." He was also an effective precinct committeeman on the North End for many years.

As you will read later, he was one of the major factors in bringing Devereux into the city—a monumental achievement for that small community. If for no other reason than that Vince Galassi would be remembered.

After his wife Mary passed away in her 50s, Vince built an apartment building on the site of the salvage yard and lived there himself. He built a three bay garage next to it and worked on cars even in retirement.

Frank Struckel Enterprises

Another self-made businessman in the village, so I was told, was Frank Struckel—the man who owned the Wobble Inn. One fellow who seemed to have his pulse on what was happening around the village said "Struckel was even wealthier than Vince Galassi, although you couldn't tell by looking at him." His most obvious business was hauling coal, but beyond that he made most of his money in the real estate business. My source claims Struckel owned a lot of houses he rented out "as many as 25 to 30 of 'em." He laughed and ended the conversation by saying, "You wouldn't think he had anything. He just walked around in those bib overalls like everybody else. He would go down to Mardi Gras every year; that was about the only thing he spent money on."

The Insurance Man

I told Al Kenal I had been in the insurance business for the last 15 years before I retired and started to write books. That triggered his memory of John Leinbahl:

John owned this town as far as the insurance business was concerned. He would sell that life insurance with those little policies and come to our house every week or so to collect our premiums. We paid ten cents a week for each policy. I think he was with John Hancock. Could he sell.

Al was referring to the old debit plans whereby an agent would sell families small whole life plans and make a weekly round of his clients to pick up the small premiums. When I was a youngster, Tony Seitz was our John Hancock agent. The nicest and most gentle man in the world, Tony later lived in Indian Hills and was one of the ushers for years at St. Al's Church. I would be home as a toddler (yet remember this clearly) when he came over in the late '40s.

Mom would give him the premium money and he would pull off a coupon on the policy with his signature on it. He tapped me on the head as he left and handed me a sucker.

What Mr. Leinbahl was doing is what in the insurance (and also real estate) business is called "farming an area." The salesperson picks out a certain area of town that is large enough to make a living and small enough to service properly. They then make it known through personal contacts, pamphlets, and other types of promotions that they specialize in that part of town. It takes dedication and hard work to do it really well and apparently this fellow was successful.

Farming

There was some farming going on to the south of Devereux, on acreage between the village and Sangamon Avenue. That expansive field was cut in two by the C & A freight railroad track which served both Peabody #59 and the Devereux Mine. The farmer operators most recall were Steve and Mary Simko, with a large family of 12—four girls and eight boys. He farmed that area, which is now Twin Lakes. Jim Bartlett thinks "he may have farmed 100 acres or so." (He was close: it was actually 114 acres of row crops and pasture.) One of the Simko sons, Jim, later gave up farming and his brother took over. Nowadays, you leave the Devereux area on Piper Road past Neil Street. There is still unimproved land on both sides of the road in row crops each year. You'd think that would have been subdivided years ago, like Indian Hills and Twin Lakes have been.

Tom Blasko, who lived on Converse a couple blocks from me as we grew up, told me about his grandfather, John Blasko, and his small farming operation:

We spent lots of time with my grandfather at his farm in Devereux. He owned about 10 acres right where I live now [on West Street]. He worked at the mine, but during the summers when he was off work he farmed those acres. He planted corn, had some pigs, and had lots of grapes in his vineyard. I helped him sell raspberries too.

Knights of Columbus Building

The K.C. has a nice block and brick building at the very southwest end of greater Devereux at the corner of West and Neil Streets. It lies on the corner of a five-acre parcel they purchased. It was built in the early sixties and dedicated by Msgr. Al Bertman, the long-time parish priest of St. Al's. (The loyal priest came off his sick bed at St. John's

Hospital to perform the ceremony shortly before his death.) The members added on the "Pelican Room" in 1974. Many Springfield people may not know about Devereux, but lots of them have been at some function at the Devereux K.C.

That K.C. Council, which began in 1952 outside of Devereux, is now the closest thing to a community center in the area. It has a bar and a large meeting room. I suppose it can serve a hundred guests or more. I've been out there several times for various events. The last one was a family gathering as a "Celebration of Life" for my mom when she passed at the age of 102. (She was proud to be the second oldest descendant from Calascio, Italy in a website database of 20,000 descendants from that little mountain town in central Italy.)

There is a very thorough history of Council #4175 on its website. From reading it, I discovered a comprehensive description of various activities members have introduced over their 50-plus years. These have included golf tournaments, a chili cook-off, chicken fry dinners, and fish fries. It obviously has an active and enthusiastic following. Member Brad Mills added that "They had some of the best burgoos in the '60s, compliments of the Ed Kohlrus

Caterers. They cooked outdoors on the east side of the building."

Coal Mines

Of course, the biggest employers around Devereux were the coal mines. The two closest were the Chicago-Springfield and Peabody #59. Since I've devoted an entire chapter to the mine that spawned the village, I think I will let that chapter be the last word about the mines and what it was like being a miner in those days.

United Zinc and Chemical Company

Undertaking the writing of this book showed me I knew little about Devereux. Almost every day of research brought new and interesting things to light about this great little enclave of souls. But nothing was more surprising to me than to discover that a smelting plant lay just across the tracks from Devereux and that lots of its citizens worked there for years.

Here is an article from the *Illinois State Register* (February 13, 1907), explaining the beginnings of the plant. Its heading reads: ZINC SMELTER COMES HERE: BIG PLANT

WILL BE ERECTED IN SPRINGFIELD IN NEAR FUTURE TO EMPLOY TWO HUNDRED AND FIFTY MEN.

After nine months of negotiations this city has secured the United Zinc & Smelting company and a plant, costing about $125,000, will soon be erected on a thirty-acre piece of ground north of the city, donated by the Chicago-Springfield Coal company. The company's smelting plant will use one hundred tons of coal daily and this is evidence in itself that the concern is a large one, and a valuable acquisition to Springfield.

Wow, why would Devereux and his boys *give* the 30 acres to National Zinc; I thought they were good businessmen? Well, the answer is in the short article: coal. Specifically, 100 tons of it a day. The mine owners had in that factory a ready-made buyer just a couple blocks away. And, of course, the coal company acquired all that top land really cheap.

You could almost see Mr. Devereux working the city levers behind everyone's back to get a good contract. And, of course, it was a good deal for the smelter too, at least for the first decade or so of operation. Since Devereux Mine, like most, closed down for four months out of the year, it averaged around 800 tons a day in production. That meant 12.5% of that daily coal was sold to National Zinc, not bad for one customer just a stone's throw across the tracks.

It took two years for the "zinc works," as the locals called it, to become operational. From the look at the accompanying drawings (in the Appendix), it was a very large physical complex. (In some documents I've seen the company referred to as United Zinc and Chemical Co. and in other places as National Zinc Co. I'm sure it was the same company, just with a name change.)

Google tells me that "Smelting is a process of applying heat to ore in order to extract a base metal. It is a form of extractive metallurgy. It is used to extract many metals from their ores, including silver, iron, copper, and other base metals." From the name of the company, the plant smelted zinc and probably other metals from raw ore or possibly ingot. Some of the undesirable by-products were sulfuric acid, lead and other possible contaminants that today would not be allowed.

Ninety-two-year-old Gene Weyant, brother of local race car legend, Chuck Weyant of Indy 500 fame, drove me around the neighborhood that Devereux folks called "the other side of the tracks." (That was not a negative phrase, just a geographical one.) Within a few blocks of his home is the area where the former United Zinc property lies. A very rough estimate of the boundary lines is Catalina Lane on the north, Norman Road on the west, and the present Union Pacific tracks on the east.

The affable and sharp Gene said that much of that area has around six feet of ash or cinders over it to separate it from the material that lies underneath, left, presumably, by United Zinc. No houses with basements were on it, Gene went on, just trailers and commercial facilities to prevent contamination.

The Zinc Works apparently operated successfully for fifteen or more years, giving jobs to many men in the community of Devereux and the surrounding area. Although the article stated United Zinc forecasted 250 workers, a 1917 book in the Sangamon Valley Collection called the *Springfield Survey* states that the smelter had 175 employees, still one of Springfield's leading employers.

Reversals of fortune came to the smelter 20 years after the first account, according to another newspaper article in the *Illinois State Journal*, dated November 17, 1927. The ominous heading reads IS NOW FOR SALE.

The gist of the article was that the smelter ran onto hard times because the bottom had fallen out of the zinc market and also because of local labor troubles. Here is the nitty-gritty for the demise from that article: "The company established itself here on the theory that it would be cheaper to freight zinc ore to the cheap coal than to transport cheap coal to the zinc ore. . . ."

The result was that the company closed down the plant, which "had been idle and rusting out for a number of years." It decided to scrap the machinery and sell all the material it could."

It was dismantled and the hardware sold by 1928 or 1929. Surprisingly, the library showed me records that the company did not sell all its property until the 1970s. I could not find out where its corporate office was or any other smelters, so it is likely out of business for good.

One local fellow who worked for a business on the zinc work site for many years shared that the smelting company had made, among other products, glazed tiles. The acid fumes used for the glazing would blow across the property and burned away everything on the ground, leaving the whole area just a barren field. When the company he worked for came in, he said, "they blew up a bunch of tunnels used in the glazing operation." (These were actually the long, round, partially-underground furnaces used for extraction.) And that pond Brad Mills and his friend would play around— remember? This man said "not one fish or one snake ever was seen in it. You could see to the bottom because it was so clear with an eerie green color."

The 1913 sales plat for Devereux Heights used by the selling agency placed around its border drawings of amenities that would attract prospective buyers to the new development. One promotes the fact that "the mammoth plant of the National Zinc Co. [is located] right west of the [Devereux Heights] Addition." It sure looks mammoth from the likeness on the sales advertisement. Two more drawings next to the plant picture show houses touting the advantages of living in "Zinc Co. Houses half a block west of our land." So, it sounds like this plant was a major investment that likely was able to attract men eager to have skilled jobs above ground. I would assume a fairly large number of Devereuxites jumped at the chance to avoid the mines.

Another interesting aspect to this factory is that I found a land transfer from *the Illinois State Register* dated October 14, 1910, on p. 16.

Through a transfer of land sold by Mrs. Cordella S. M. Warren to George A. Wood, John McCreery, E. Sulzenstein, H.H. Devereux and J.A. Hall, and by them to the United Zinc and Chemical company, the last named concern becomes owner of eleven acres of land southeast of the city [of Springfield]. The price in both instances was $3,618.

Why the owners of the Devereux Coal Mine would purchase 11 acres on the southeast edge of the city to immediately resell to United Zinc is interesting. Why not purchase it directly? Notice that the seller was the same person who sold her land to Devereux for the mine and the addition.

Piper Road Service Station & Civic Center

During the late 1920s or early 1930s, Vince Galassi's father owned a filling (gas) station just south of Piper School and across the road (in front of his residence). I had never heard of this even after interviewing over a dozen villagers until Vince's daughters related it to me. That's not surprising because hardly anyone is alive from that time. The Galassi girls told me about it because their dad had told them. Here's the way their story went.

Michael and Ubalda Galassi were from Purello, Italy. He was a coal miner at nearby Peabody #59, and they lived on Piper Road with their six children. Vince was the only boy. They lived in one of the two upstairs apartments. Being an entrepreneur himself, Michael rented out the extra apartment next to theirs and the bottom floor too. That served as a dancehall and sometimes as a community center and meeting hall.

Michael's gas station had one of those hand pumps with a glass cylinder where you could see the gasoline inside.

All was going well for a few years. Then the Coal Miner Union War came to central Illinois. The Sangamon County History website encapsulates the drama in one riveting sentence:

A bitter battle between rival coal mine unions, a battle that began and effectively ended in Springfield, led to strikes, bombings, street riots and at least six killings in Sangamon County in the 1930s.

Since Galassi was aligned with the fiery John L. Lewis and his UMWA (United Mine Workers of America), the aggrieved "Progressives" (with the Progressive Miners Association) took to the streets and one night came looking for the enemy at Galassi's side business, Devereux's lone gas station. The girls continued:

"Those Progressives took their revenge on him. One night they came by and threw a Molotov cocktail at the gas station. They missed it, but hit the first floor of his house/meeting room, causing enough damage that he hired a night watchman after that." That was around 1931 or 1932.

The Hub Clothier Baseball Team c. 1932. From left to right. Top
row: Willie Burge, Frank Barlick, Louie Barlick, Sam LaFuria,
Dolcido Micheletti, Fred Bedolli, Joe Beja and Raymond Favero.
Middle Row: Bowser Viele, Art Cooke, Harry Potish (owner?), Gus
Ozellis, Marino Paoni and son Leo, Vincent Rondelli, and Frank
Tomasavich (Manager). Front Row: John Paoni, Lyndo Fazi, Irwin
Potish (child), John Rondelli, and Victor Kinzora. (Courtesy Jim &
Nancy Bartlett)

Chapter Six

The Village People

There is no village without inhabitants. Even with people it has no history without their stories. And the stories are meaningless unless they are brought to life with detailed, remembered images and honest, real-life drama.

Therefore, I wanted to talk to as many people as I could who live in Devereux or grew up in or near the little burg. Most of all I wanted to talk to relatives or friends of those who moved into that area when it was all lots and no houses. I wanted to hear stories from across the 116 years span of time—from every one of the 11 decades Devereux Heights has experienced. That was my objective. I may not have been able to capture the entire length of that time period, but I sure tried. And I received some good stories to share with you.

I was hopeful that the bulk of this book was those stories. That didn't happen, but what follows is at least a collection of what I could gather (within time restraints) from Northenders who wanted those stories to be shared and, most of all, remembered.

This chapter will describe typical village scenes and how townspeople went about their daily lives. I tried to answer the question "What was it like and what were they like back then?" This chapter will be a peek inside daily lives and how people lived their lives. The next chapter will recognize the more intimate aspects of their lives. Where this chapter is a view from the street, the next chapter will be a view into their living rooms, so to speak.

Bench Talk— by Rudy Rodolfi

I want to begin the stories of real peoples' lives by recounting this wonderful picture that, if any mental image can, encapsulates the essence of that community in its early days. Rudy related this story to me, and it was verified by others too. It seems as though the women of the village, after a long day of hard work cooking, cleaning, childrearing, etc., would find time some evenings after supper to relax a bit.

Most houses on Angelo Street (and I assume the others as well) had picket fences or some other defined barrier in the front, near the street. In front of the fence at most residences would be a long, wooden bench where women would gather. They were simply 3"x12"x12' rough pieces of lumber supported by bricks or blocks, nothing fancy. (They were similar to the one in front of the Jailhouse Tavern, which is pictured elsewhere in this book.) The children would be playing near them in the yard or street, such as hide-and-seek or kick the can.

So, one woman [Rudy began] *may holler to, or motion at, her neighbor lady friends that they should come sit with her tonight. Several could sit comfortably on the long benches. (The Jailhouse had an especially long one in front of it.) On another night, another woman would have her friends over at her bench. And on and on.*

Can't you just close your eyes and go back in time to see this evening ritual play out? That scene in my mind's eye shows the Italian ladies in their faded print dresses and clean aprons and hair in buns, high socks, and black shoes on. (I see that image because that's exactly how my own wonderful Grandma Roscetti looked in those clothes. I saw her like that in her kitchen almost every day of my young life, living four houses down from her and Grandpa.)

It was probably an hour of glorious relaxation, laughing and talking about the kids plus local gossiping. Then they had to break it off and return to their chores—cleaning up, making their husbands' lunches for the next day, giving the kids baths, and other never-ending chores.

How I would love to get ahold of one of those benches. I asked everyone I interviewed if they know who has one, but no luck so far.

For those captured moments, those women had a little bit of deserved respite in Devereux Heights, Illinois. . . and created memories that lasted their lifetimes. And now, maybe with you reading this, they will continue to last even longer in our collective memories.

Guys' Time Out – by Al Kenal

Al "Luke" Kenal, during our meeting along with his daughter, Karen, in his home on Angelo Street, kept emphasizing the bond formed by the townspeople of Devereux. One example of his was neighbor men getting together in the evening after a hard day's work—the men's bench time, so to speak. Here's his recollection:

You might have a group of men—mostly miners—build a big bonfire in somebody's back yard and just sit around it, talking. They'd often have it next door to my dad's house, in Charlie Bedolli's grandfather's yard. They would ask me or some other kids to run down to the Jailhouse Tavern and get them a jug of beer. The bartender knew who it was for and so filled the jug with draft beer. It was fun hearing the men talk and laugh and tell stories at their fire chats during the summer months.

Al mentioned that community ritual which I had not heard before. It was one of several examples Al used to emphasize the fellowship of their tight community. Here's another he remembers.

When people died in Devereux, several women around town would take up a collection of flowers and sometimes money for the decedent's family. Often it was Helen "H" Sefick or my mother, Mary. [Sophie Geyston and Betty Hickman also helped, others told me.] They made a detailed listing of everyone who contributed and gave that to the family too. It was just something that was routinely done.

Gladys Sefick piggybacked on Al's reminiscences. She was married to "H's" son, John, and so brings these memories through them:

Helen, Olga Handley, and Sophie Geyston also took care of the food when somebody died. They would prepare it, then bring it to the hall [the KC building or at St. Al's basement], and lay it all out. In addition, they would maintain the buffet as people ate the food. They did it all, those women.

When Helen died, I remember that Sophie brought a book to the reception that listed all the people who had died and with each one a list of who gave what. She had that list going way back.

Services Missing in Devereaux

That brings up a topic connected to the above ritual. There were at least three essential institutions that all towns usually have that were conspicuously lacking in Devereux. One was a cemetery—my thought from the last memory, about St. Al's Church. Instead, they buried their dead in Calvary Cemetery since most of the town was Italian and therefore Catholic. It was located three miles away on the west side of Lincoln Park, next to Oak Ridge Cemetery where Abraham Lincoln is interred.

They also did not have a church. I don't know where townspeople worshiped in those first couple of decades. Most probably didn't go, but those who were dedicated enough may have walked the two-plus miles to the St. Francis Chapel at the Mother House near Riverton. August 1, 1928 was a red letter date for Catholic families all around the North End. A new parish formed on Sangamon Avenue and 20th Street. St. Aloysius Church was at first four portable buildings donated by the local school board. They were also used for the school that started that fall. Two years later they built a place to worship and learn in a permanent structure. St. Aloysius church and school have served Devereux and other North-End neighborhoods ever since. (I remember the day in 1955 when our St. Al's teachers allowed the entire student body to stand outside and watch a crane place the steeple in place on our brand-new church, allowing the adjacent school building more room for classrooms.)

The third very important service that was lacking in the village was a doctor. Rudy enlightened me that Dr.

Sterbini, an Italian physician, was the doctor of choice for Devereux folks. His office was in downtown Springfield in the Kerasotes building at 6th & Washington (across the street from Frascos' Italian-American Import Store). However, Rudy continued, "Dr. Sterbini made house calls, as was the custom of that era. There may have also been a Dr. Rossi, but I can't remember anything about him but the name." (Nor could I find anything about a Dr. Rossi.) It is certain that there were several women who helped in childbirth. Midwives was another product of the time and of course births occurred almost exclusively in the family homes.

Convenient Rides: The Interurban

Springfield was one of the hubs of an interurban rail line, formally called the Illinois Traction System. The Sangamon County History website describes it as providing "frequent, cheap, and comfortable transportation to people who, prior to widespread automobile access, had no other convenient way of getting from town to town." The train's early distinction was its power source: it was 'tractioned' by an electric line above the pull car."

Using the "flag stop" method (i.e., waving down the train to stop for you), Devereux residents as well as visitors were able to hop a ride on the electric railway or the "car line," as it was commonly called, to a number of cities around the state. It linked up with St. Louis, Springfield, Champaign, Danville, Bloomington-Normal, and Peoria.

Dominic Giacomini told me he would take it to Bradley University on a regular basis. He and others would have found it most convenient since it ran right along Devereux, on the west-most street in town, aptly named Interurban Avenue. It served these various communities on its 550 miles of rail for over 50 years, from 1901 in some places until the mid-1950s in others.

You'll read in the next chapter about how Rudy Rodolfi would return to Springfield from her job at Caterpillar in Peoria almost every weekend to help her ailing parents and errant brother. She took the convenient Interurban train which lived up to its reputation of affordable fares: the round-trip cost her all of $2.87.

A Local Character— by Charlie Bedolli

When writing about a town or neighborhood or company, I always want to find out about the local characters—those colorful people who stand out for one reason or another. It may be their charm, their eccentricities, their larger-than-life personas. Same went for this village.

Charlie Bedolli shared the story of a man selling brooms throughout the village. He would come through every once in a while, trying to hawk his wares, which included brooms as his lead product, from a wagon.

Charlie's grandfather would invite the man to stop by his house. The vendor held himself out as an Indian, but he may have been black. Mr. Bedolli would get him "pickled" on his red wine and eventually get a free broom out of the deal.

Grapes, Arbors & Vineyards

Sitting in their garage at the end of Angelo Street one warm day this summer, Bob and Mary Yoggerst invited their next door neighbor, Charlie Bedolli, to join us. We talked about a number of subjects when somebody pointed to the Temperelli house across the street and said, "Boy, did Henry make the wine."

Most everybody in the village drank homemade wine throughout the year—Prohibition or not. (You could make and consume wine legally, even during the '20s, as long as it was within certain volume limits.) And some, like Temperelli, made a lot of it during normal times. He would get a big shipment and shovel all those grapes into his basement window. Charlie's grandfather would make eight 50 gallon barrels of wine a year plus another barrel of wine vinegar for salad dressing. ("He'd bury that barrel under sand so the sunlight wouldn't interfere with the fermentation, so it'd stay vinegary.")

Many central Illinois citizens didn't know it, but Devereux was one of the biggest wine-making communities around. There were vineyards on almost every lot. Moreover, some folks went in together and would order an *entire* hopper car of California grapes each season. Mrs. Gallo's family, from her farm on Mayden Avenue, made a lot of it. [Perhaps the Gallos owned the Mayden property before the Maydens, but I haven't been able to verify that.] The Barn Tavern sold some of it. They would even sell it to the Italian-American Import Store on 6th Street in downtown Springfield. But most folks made their own wine from Italian grapes—blue, red and yellow varieties.

Jim Galassi, when the subject of wine came up, said,

You know how kids go around and pick grapes from the vineyards in peoples' backyards? Well, you didn't do that in Devereux. No even one grape, or you were in big trouble!" That says it all about wine-making in the village.

Al Kenal said people normally made decent wine from their own grapes, which of course had come from the Old Country when people immigrated. "But if they wanted to have top notch wine for special occasions or for guests, they would order California grapes by truck and take their individual crates home, like Temperelli."

"Play Ball!"— by Rudy Rodolfi

Rudy told me about the sport she loved and was lucky to play for close to 20 years—baseball, or in her case, softball. To my question, "Were there ball teams around Devereux?" She answered with excitement:

The only team I remember that was all village people was the Hub Clothiers men's baseball team. Vince "Chow" Rondell and his brother "Punch" were pitchers. There was also "Skets" Galassi and "Beeb" Bedolli.

We did have one women's softball team sponsored by the Salvation Army and coached by Fred "Snooks" Paoni. I recall some local girl on it, a player by the name of Elenore "Rudy" Rodalfi! [She told me with a wink and a smile] *There were also Viola "Toni" Galassi and Dorothy (Paoni) Gentry.*

The Loveable Miscreant— by Merino Giacomini

Joe wasn't his real name, but that's what I'll call him. Joe liked his booze. I wouldn't describe him as a true alcoholic nor even as the village drunk. Like I said, he just liked his booze. His specialty was whiskey, but if it wasn't available, wine or beer would suffice. He was undoubtedly the kindest, most generous man whom I had ever had the distinct pleasure of knowing. If anyone needed something done or needed help doing it, Joe would be right there with a helping hand. He actually found pleasure in doing things for people.

As teenagers, we really didn't have much to keep us entertained in Devereaux Heights. We had a grocery store and a tavern next door called the "Jail House Tavern." The building which housed the tavern was once a combination garage and storage area. The three windows on the front had vertical steel bars spaced about ten inches apart, just enough to keep the thieves out. Hence the reason for the name. The façade resembled an old jail house in some western movie.

I had to stay home every night of the week except Saturday nights. On that glorious night, my best friend, Al Gentry, and I would head for the Jail House to sit on the bench that lined the front of the tavern. My mom always gave me fifteen or twenty cents to spend. I think Al's mom give him about the same amount. Most of the other occupants of the benches were six to ten years older than Al and me. Most of them had jobs and some money in their pockets. Al and I would wait as long as we could stand it, and then finally we would go in and treat ourselves to a Pepsi and a Mars Bar. The Pepsi cost ten cents and the Mars Bar a nickel. We would nurse our treat for as long as possible, for we knew that that was it until the next Saturday.

On this one particular Saturday night, my friend Al and I observed old Joe sitting on the bench in front of the tavern. He had half of a watermelon sliced the long way, laying across his lap. He pulled a fork out of his bib overalls' pocket and started to punch holes in the heart of the melon.

He then reached into his back pocket, pulled out a half pint of his favorite whiskey and poured it across the length of the melon. Joe had just transformed the watermelon into a "whiskey melon." With the metamorphosis completed, Joe dug in. I learned something that day. I found that it really didn't take much to make some people happy, at least not for good old Joe.

A Most Interesting Character— by Rudy Rodolfi

The person that came to mind first when you asked me if I knew "any real characters" in Devereux growing up was, without a hesitation, my recollection of Severio "Pepo" Galassi. By the time I recall him, he had long since retired from the mine, and so all his days were free to do what he wanted. He was in his seventies by then. His wife's name was Santina. His son and daughter may have helped support their parents at that point , but I'm not sure.

What I recall is that every morning he would place on his shoulder a long pole with a gunnysack tied to the end and balance that with one hand and carry a long-handled axe with the other. He would go to the freight train track where the coal cars went on and start walking north. My guess is that he went all the way to the river and maybe beyond it.

A little before noon, Mr. Galassi would return with his quarry. It might consist of some lumps of coal, an old beat-up pan with cigarette butts in it, and maybe a catfish or carp. (He made his own fishing pole out of a tree branch, a shoestring for the line, and a safety pin for the hook.)

He always brought back a small tree that he cut down with the axe and trimmed the branches off of it. He would pull it behind him as he walked. One thing I found interesting was he cut the four to six -nch tree on a precise angle and then cut the other end to match. He would later cut it in lengths for firewood. Since he did that most every day, he had the biggest wood pile in the village. And what amazed me was that every piece of firewood was the same length and stacked in neat rows. He was something, that "Pepo."

I found that recollection so interesting because it reminds me of my own grandfather. As a small boy, I would see him walking around the neighborhood—usually in the alleys—with his cane, picking up odd things like "Pepo" did. Grandpa would wear a big brim straw hat, an Army surplus green shirt buttoned up to his neck, baggy tan pants cinched tight, and work shoes, what we called clodhoppers. He loved "junking it," as my friends called what he did.

Devereux's Reputation: KEEP OUT

I thought of my second-grade teacher one day some years back and decided to see if she was still with us. She answered the phone in a spritely manner, so I asked her to lunch for old times' sake. Sister Louise (Gietl) remembered my sister but not me, she recalled over a Cobb salad I bought her. The only other conversation piece I remember—and this is my point—was a reference to Devereux. "Ken," she said with the kind of honesty I would expect from a religious person, "the other sisters around town used to feel sorry for us Ursulines at St. Al's because 'you had those mean Devereux boys.'"

I laughed at that slight, thinking my schoolmates from Devereux didn't seem bad in the least. I must have pushed that comment way down in my brain's basement because I never thought about it again until the day I interviewed Jim and Nancy Bartlett. Here's Nancy take on the topic:

Before the war [WWII] there were lots of teenage boys around here. And let me tell you, they were tough! You used to hear people say that "those Devereux kids are mean" and they were. When I went to Ursuline Academy, I was even pushed out a group of ten girls because I was from Devereux. Their parents told their daughters "don't hang around them because they are bad people."

While still working on his morning cheese sandwich, Jim then drew into the conversation:

One day when we were around some Springfield kids, this one boy looked me up and down and said, "You don't look that tough." Another time my brother and I walked by the coal chutes and some other boys from Devereux even beat us up.

Nancy then mentioned a fight at the Roll Inn Tavern.

My mom, who was very young at the time, was at a dance there and a guy made eyes at this woman. One of the local boys went over and hit him so hard, he landed in the big drum on the band stage. He said something to the effect, "Don't mess with our girls."

After hearing these comments, I reflected on my dad talking about the "Rabbit Row" kids in his neighborhood (south of present day Lanphier High School). He told me they were pretty rough themselves, always fighting kids from other neighborhoods. So, my conclusion is that neighborhoods in those days (and even nowadays in some areas) are like gangs in that they protect their own turf and stick up for each other.

This especially went for Devereux, which was out in the sticks in those days, an enclave, not close to other neighborhoods. The people took care of themselves and each other to the detriment of outsiders. The boys taught themselves self-reliance, rugged individualism. They were handy, smart, and resourceful and so figured things out in that relative isolation. And that included the necessity of being tough.

Bill Shay has lived in Devereux for the past 30 years. Before that, he was friends with kids from the village and he attended St. Al's, which had Devereux kids too. He summed up the way outsiders—at least street-smart ones—understood things here: "You didn't come out here unless you were invited . . . If you knew what was good for you." Simple as that.

The subject of Devereux having some roughians in it made me smile after reading a blog (Legends of America) about some mining towns. Referring to Braidwood, Illinois, where coal was first discovered in Illinois by a farmer while digging a well in 1872, the blogger states that it had "the reputation as a wild town full of transients, tramps and thieves." Compared to mining towns such as that, Devereux was not all that bad. But they were bad enough. Al Kenal remarked on the subject that kids in the old days (1920s and 1930s) referred to their patch and their reputation in it with the exaggerated moniker, "Bucket of Blood."

The Unspeakable: Intermarriage

My mother was among four sisters who grew up in an all Italian family in an (almost) all Italian mining community. There were just two non-Italian families in Starnes, a tiny village on the northeast edge of Grandview.

So Mom, as well as Aunts Claudia, Elynore and Florence understood they were to marry with "their own kind." All but Florence broke the mold and married "Johnnie Bulls," or men of English descent. Florence did something worse: she married a Sicilian—what my grandfather derisively dubbed "Bumblebee Dagos." For some reason I have never been able to find out.

He disliked men from that island province because (he said) they gave regular Italians a bad name, since Sicilians had the reputation as gangsters and Mafiosos.

Rudy Rodolfi shared with me that her father expressed the same sentiments, which were common among the other Italian villagers of Devereux. "Dad thought Sicilians were bad guys and wanted us to keep our distance from them. Of course, never date or marry one. In addition, he disliked other Italians which he felt were beneath them, which he collectively termed *Brusezzi*. He said they were from the Bologna area, the norther part of Italy."

By contrast, most of the village folks were from Central Italy, from the region called Umbria—towns like Perugia, Gubbio, and Purello.

In the early days these mining families—both Italian and other Europeans—wanted their children to stay pure and marry within their own nationalities.

Naturally, as time went on and children grew up together, played together and attended school together, mixing of the various countries became inevitable and problematic for the parents. You can imagine how the parents besmirched other nationality traits. Heck, we still have some of that today.

Nowadays, in Devereux and wherever else the original miners' progeny have migrated to, there are Italian-Polish, Italian-German, Italian-Austrians, etc. For that time, and probably through the 1940s, it made for awkward conversations around many Thanksgiving dinner tables.

The Strong-willed Pasquale Fofi

One elderly person related this story which is now passed on as true village lore. Tireless Father Al Bertman, the priest at the new St. Aloysius parish, was an active community leader, a parish priest, and a proselytizer. In that last capacity the young, eager-beaver parson was about the business of saving souls. There were lots of souls in the little burg of Devereux Heights he noticed early on, and so he focused on them as his first project.

Father Al would hold what amounted to mini-revival meetings in the very visible Paoni front yard on the most trafficked road in Devereux. He did this for several years after the war, to increase the size of his parish. Mrs. Paoni would set up 30 or more folding chairs to help the priest. Following impassioned sermons, the young priest would set about the conversion process. Once he converted enough new Catholics, he would also arrange for formal instructions there.

He converted a lot of people [this lady started] *that way. One day in particular, Father Al was holding a catechism class in the front yard of the Paoni house. There was a small crowd in addition to the converts. All of a sudden, short Mr. Fofi walks out of the grocery store's side door and rushes over to his house next door. He was so mad at the priest for using his neighbor's yard—and the village—as a place for that stuff. For some reason, even as an Italian, he hated Catholics. He cussed the baffled priest out in Italian. After his tirade was over and he went back into his store, Father Al told the people, "He doesn't think I know what he was saying, but I do."*

After I discussed this episode with Rudy one day, she interjected her father's strong feelings about Father Al and the Church:

My dad would make us kids come in the house when Father Al was seen coming around. He didn't want him trying to get us coming to church or having anything to do with religion. He told us, "When you grow up, you can make up your own mind." He didn't even want us baptized, although Mom took care of that behind his back.

Mr. Fofi also [this first source above continued] *had no love lost for people of English ancestry either. He called them "Johnnie Bull," a sharply negative term for those descendants.*

I sure understood that because my grandfather would sometimes remind me that I was half "Johnnie Bull," adding that "[They are] not too smart." I was puzzled by that comment but never said anything to him about what I took as a personal affront.

Common Pastime Games

One of the games kids played we called rutzela, Dominic Giacomini explained, *is where someone would roll a wooden wheel and keep pushing it down the street. They would wind string around the wheel so it would move straight in the middle of the street. The person who rolled it the farthest won.*

Al Kenal mentioned that men played *rutzela* almost as much as bocce ball (below). They interjected beer into it, of course. He added to what Nick said above:

They made the wheel by cutting a 7" or 8" diameter tree trunk or branch about 1-1/2 inches thick. Then they would often soak it—elm was the preferred wood—and add a strip of leather around the outer part of the wheel. They sometimes placed a piece of lead in the middle for balance I suppose. To roll it, the player would wind a piece of heavy fish cord around his throwing hand and with the remainder of the three-foot cord, he would wind it around the circumference of the wheel. The player rolled it as far as he could. One man rolled it down Interurban and right through the front wheel of a motorcycle on the By-pass.

The most popular game which men played during the early days of Devereux and into the fifties was bocce ball. I usually associate it with old men because we kids would watch them play it on a court next to Trello's Tavern on 19th and Cummins, right next to the railroad tracks. I notice it has had a resurgence today, with courts in Lincoln and Rotary Parks, and maybe others. I even saw people play it at a popular downtown tavern recently.

Bob and Mary Yoggerst, along with Nick, explained the game:

They played it all over town. Of course, they had games and tournaments at the Jailhouse and the Roll Inn. But they would play it mostly in the streets. They'd have a game at one end of the block and then move down a ways and play another game and just keep moving all day.

Since I know nothing about the game—and you may not either—here are the basics, as they were explained to me. As I understand it, there are two teams with four men on a side (sometimes up to six). One point is given to each bocce ball that is closer to the pallino than the other team's balls. (A pallino is a smaller ball, used as the target ball.) The game continues until one side has 21 points (in their Old Country way of scoring).

The interesting part of the game, which I suppose is not regulation, was that in Devereux the losing team had to buy the winning players each a 10-cent glass of beer. You can see that this rule lead to some interesting afternoons among those old gents.

Al Kenal added that the men would try to end up at the Jailhouse Tavern, so the losers could buy the winners beer.

Loren Martin, who grew up in the area, told me as we sat at the bar in Pam's Jailhouse Tavern the other day, that "when I was just a kid I would see the old guys playing bocce ball in front here [pointing to the door] and about 20 others under the tree across the street drinking and laughing and having a good old time watching the game they just finished down the streets."

Another pastime for the neighborhood boys was playing in the woods on the southwest edge of town (on the west side of the tracks) everybody called "Hobo Jungle." It was several acres of trees and brush just down the tracks from the C & A coal chute.

The coal chute was an awkward-looking concrete structure that was manned by three railroad workers. It was their job to resupply coal to the tender, the car right behind the steam engine, before going on to Springfield. Its other job, just as critical, was supplying the train engines with water to generate the steam. To obtain enough water for several trains a day, the railroad company ran a pipe from the Sangamon River (at the old dam on Paint Road) all the way to the chute, which was two or three miles, as the crow flies.

Hobo Jungle was the default destination for boys if fun things were slow in the village. Its name is derived from the fact that vagrants or tramps would jump off the trains at that concealed area before they moved on to Springfield, where railroad detectives could arrest them for trespass. (Jim Bartlett interjected that "those railroad police could be really mean.")

In my short memoir *Converse Kids: Growing Up in the Fifties*, I talk about how we would walk the tracks from around 15th and Keys all the way up to that area, which we called by the same name. It was a leisurely stroll of about 20 minutes that would give us something to do in the summers that seemed adventurous. We were hoping to find some hobos there, yet scared to death if we did. All we ever came across were their campsites, with open cans, discarded clothing, and dead campfires.

As another quick aside, our gang of kids' default adventure site was "the cotton woods," a one-acre refuge (at Michigan and Black Avenue) we called our own and played in it much of the summers. We made forts and had fun hiding out from the world. Right north of it was the "old paint factory." Part of it was torn down and we would gingerly walk above the ten-foot basement on the narrow foundation ledges. On the tracks that used to serve the plant were parked train cars. Most of my friends walked from box car to box car, jumping from one to the other. Not me. It had a poor risk-reward ratio, to this young mind. The reason I mention our little world is because I'm sure some Devereux kids came down our way to explore these areas, like we explored theirs surreptitiously. Funny, but we never crossed paths.

Depression Years in the Patch

The economic turndown throughout the 1930s and until the war years was a national catastrophe for most Americans. It hit Devereuxites particularly hard because of the mines being closed all summer and exacerbated by the mine wars. One long-time denizen put it in a personal perspective:

Lots of guys went to prison for stealing in Devereux. Everything from wine to chickens. . . anything not tied down.

They were desperate. The police put them in jail—they didn't mess around.

Carpenter Park Picnics

The Bartletts expressed surprise when they told me about the summer parties out at Carpenter's Park, a pastime I had not heard from anybody else I interviewed up to that point. (All subjects don't just sprout up organically during the interview process. Prodding must be enjoined.)

I woke up and prodded and they responded thus:

There was a shelter and firepit right when you drove up to the park. Every summer after the war [WWII] Devereux people would organize a big party there. It was a big affair, with food, beer and polka dancing. Hotdogs were among the celebrated food. Everybody from the village would be out there—adults and their kids. It was a big affair for many years.

Another serial attendee told me that "we took care to pick everything up when we left. You, know, leave it better than we found it? One of our values was not only cleanliness but respect for the park." I liked that little bit of extra civility. Maybe it was because they didn't have a park of their own in the village.

River Camp No. Four—by Al Kenal

For many years, a group of ten men from Devereux maintained a unique bond formed around a cabin along the Sangamon River. The beginning of this story is when several men from the village just decided that they should form a fishing club of sorts.

They laid out a few rules (such as, the club was restricted to 10 members and their kids and friends could not go down there at night by themselves) and rented one of the cabins, called Camp No. 4. The site was located on the south shore of the river, just off of U.S. Route 55, a couple of miles east of Devereux. They rented on a yearly basis one of the six cabins owned by Kate Radford and her husband. (He passed away shortly after the cabin rental business began, leaving Kate in charge.)

The Radfords had a few acres where they pastured their cattle and built a cluster of six cabins—what everyone referred to as camps—for a little added revenue. They rented them out to mainly weekenders who wanted to get away from it all and enjoy the outdoors, especially by fishing.

The Devereux men used the camp mostly for fishing. But a few times each year they would have big parties and invite friends and families. The themes would be around either burgoo or chicken. Beer kegs were a central feature of any get-together. There would be laughter, horseshoes, eating and drinking among all who attended. But most of the time, it was just one or more club members who would get away to the cabin for the fishing and friendship.

Right in the middle was Camp #4, and it was the best campsite, Al Kenal explained to me. It was high enough to avoid flooding, yet close enough to the river and their dock. They had a decent cabin with a water tank on the side. Nearby was their "hacienda," a closed-in structure with screened-in windows and doors when the mosquitos were bad.

Al told me his dad and the other guys made use of their camp for over 40 years. Among this tight group of friends were his dad, his uncle Joe Galassi, Ray Beul, Beeb Bedolli, Louis Simko, Toots Sefick and John Randelli—and eventually Al himself.

"Dad and Toots [Al explained] would sometimes spend their entire two-week vacations there, together, fishing and talking their time away. When Dad came home, he smelled bad—there was no place to bathe but the river itself."

Finally, someone bought the land from a tired Kate, tore down her cabins, and built a house back there. But all those years of memories—they lasted and are now recorded permanently.

Pond Life— By Brad Mills

Brad answered my question about ponds in the area. I happen to love them. I fell in love with ponds and their life forms while fishing with my dad as a young boy. Dad had the ability to talk farmers into allowing him to fish (and also hunt) on their places. I especially took to the microscopic life in ponds and constructed in my basement a lab equipped with a microscope, beakers, flasks and other paraphernalia. In college I took a course in water biology. So, it is a subject I like to explore with the people I spoke with. Most people didn't know of any close-by water holes, but Brad mentioned three.

Right near Hobo Jungle was a small pond, probably no bigger than someone's backyard swimming pool. "You could get to it one of two ways," Brad Mills explained, as he drew me a small map." Across Interurban Avenue and Mayden was a trail across the track. You could use that and then walk south aways. The more direct route was to take the drainage tunnel close to Hobo Jungle and walk a ways to it. Through those woods there was a shallow draw that added to the adventure of being in the thick of things."

Brad became more animated when he told me about an incident that occurred at that pond:

All us kids decided to dig the pond deeper. It was pretty shallow. So, one kid gets a shovel and starts digging up the mud and throwing it on the bank. When he pulls up the shovel the second time a big ole' snake was on the shaft, all curled around it. He threw it down and we all ran away.

Up a few blocks and just north of where Donna Street runs into Interurban Avenue, there was a larger pond, about the size of half a football field. The kids called it "Devereux Pond" even though, like Hobo Jungle and that small pond, it lay across the tracks on a commercial property. It was not a fishing pond at all. In fact, it was a greenish color that "didn't look as though anything could live in it." Still, Brad and his buddies would play around it and use it for ice hockey in the winter. Lou Menendez confessed to me that he and his buddies actually swam in it a few times. "Most of the guys who did are dead now. Bad stuff. It killed 'em. But I'm still alive."

The third pond Brad mentioned was at the Jones & Adams Mine southeast of Devereux at the north end of Peerless Mine Road. That mine had been closed due to a fire in the '50s. Its slag pile was still there as well as a deep hole in the ground filled with water ("where two box cars could have stood up length-wise and still be under the water, was the rumor!"). They did fish and swim in that mine pond. It had a lot of fish in it. And especially frogs.

Watercress & Bluebells—by Rudy Rodolfi

We used to walk up Donna Street and then on the [east] *railroad track and have picnics with our friends there, close to where the [Devereux] mine had been. We called it Catchfire for some reason. It was a nice little area where we would sit around and talk and maybe bring sandwiches.*

We also enjoyed going to the "The Spring," a nice little creek across the Bypass, maybe 200 yards farther north. Nobody bothered us there. I remember we would gather up watercress, clean it off and eat it. Farther up still, by the river, we also had fun. It was just trees and prairie with lots of Bluebell flowers, so we christened this other sanctuary "Blue Valley Inn."

Nicknames

Mary Yoggerst announced to me during our first interview in her home (with Dominic Giacomini and Bob present) that "practically every boy, man and woman in Devereux had a nickname. Most people never knew what their real names were."

The first name that came to my mind was my schoolmate John Sefick, whom we all called "Fibber." The only reason I knew his real first name was because the nuns called on him in class by John. Al Kenal told me how he got his nickname, that stuck with him most of his life:

Uncle Joe noticed that John and his cousin Patty Huffman were inseparable as kids and decided to name them "Fibber" and "Molly," after the radio show "Fibber McGee & Molly." His stayed with him, but Patty's parents hated her nickname and nixed it.

164

Al told me that after I asked him if the rumor was true that Devereux folks all had nicknames to maintain their anonymity during Prohibition Days. He said that was not true and told me the above story to prove his point. But others swear by the rumor, which has some logic to it.

Here is a rendition of some of the names Bob and Mary blurted out to me off the top of their heads: "Frog" (John Paoni), "Gip" (John Golab), "Casey Jones" (Charlie Bedolli's uncle).

Then there was "Wob" Sefick, "Snooks" (Fred Paoni), "Skeets" (Joe Paoni), "Panny" (Joe F.), "Punch" (Rondelli), "Coon" (Micheletti), and then more Paoni names—"Rab," Razz" and "Doc," on and on. Not as many girls seemed to be blessed with bynames, but there were some. "H" comes to mind—Helen Sefick, that's one. Two others were Sophia Geyston ("Polly") and Josephine Paciorek ("Nanny").

A Village Pox: Excess Drinking

There was lots of drinking in Devereux as there was in any mining community. My mother told me about men in Starnes—even her father—who drank to excess routinely. You can almost understand why: backbreaking labor, horrible working conditions, discrimination, meager wages. Men could barely provide for their families. Alcohol was to many an outlet, an anesthesia to dull their stark realities. I won't identify the two men whom several people brought up in interviews. Suffice it to say these were extreme cases that give you an idea how pervasive overdrinking was in general.

One fellow was given the nickname of Mayor. When I asked the interviewee why, he responded in a way that startled me:

He was a really smart guy, but he spent most of his life on a barstool in the Jailhouse Tavern. . . and that was basically our townhall, hence we called him "mayor" since he presided there daily and nightly.

Another town alcoholic drank so much he often could be seen walking so off kilter you'd think he would simply fall over. He sometimes would literally crawl on his hands and knees from the Jailhouse to his home, a quarter mile down the road. One observer remembers this fellow at one of the river parties:

I swear, I watched him the whole night, just sitting there drinking. He never once ate one scrap of food, nor did he once go to the bathroom. All he did was drink for two or three hours straight. I never saw anything like that. . . He was known for drinking an entire case of bottled beer every damn night at the tavern.

Wasted lives, is the sad thought that came to my mind as I listened to these tragic stories. Unfortunately, alcoholism seems to be a part of almost every extended family, even (or especially) today. Like any small town, it is an example of ordinary life in microcosm; thus, it is more readily apparent to us in close proximity to one's neighbor, as in the village of Devereux.

The KKK Paid Visits to the Village

In the late teens and early 1920s the KKK would pay visits to Devereux. Not a lot, but several times. One senior citizen told me his parents related this story to him. The Ku Klux Klan was reputed to have had some meetings in the Devereux area.

My parents told me they met one time in that depression on the south side of the road between Mayden Avenue and Piper Road. That ditch was pretty deep, as well as wide. I suppose it was 10 feet down and probably 20 feet wide. Sometimes, drunks would end up driving in it.

"Dago Hill"

"Dago" is normally taken as a derisive swipe at Italians. But in my Italian family (Roscettis, Antonaccis, Capronicas and Cellinis), it was freely used with no repercussions. Maybe it's like some blacks referring to themselves by the N-word—acceptable by the group but anathema for outsiders to use. ("Wop" was a different story.)

The same nonchalant attitude applied in Devereux since an entire street was given the colloquial name, "Dago Hill." Probably 90 percent of the whole early community was Italian. The others were mainly Polish, Slavs and German.

This east-most road in Devereux, as all the others, did not use its legal name (East Street) nor its adopted name (Angelo Street) until after 1967. It was from time immemorial called "Dago Hill." It was filled with Italian families as you will shortly read. It was also actually a hill, climbing noticeably from its origin at Mayden Avenue north to its terminus at Randy Street at a seven-degree grade, with a hic-up in the middle for a passing stream under the road.

Anyway, to give you an idea how Italian "Dago Hill" was populated, Rudy was kind enough to supply me with as many family names as she could remember. She and her family lived on it too: she blurted, "R.R. 5, Box 64."

Before naming all her neighbors, she mentioned the only three residents north of Angelo Street: Mr. & Mrs. Ganz, on the northern-most street (which had no name but is now called Magdalena Street); Mr. & Mrs. Dumbris lived on North Street (now Randy), just east of the ravine and tracks, and just south of the Ganz family; and Felix & Mary Golab lived in the only house (at the time) on what was left of East Street.

Now, here Rudy, exercising her memory muscles, goes on reciting all the neighbors on "Dago Hill," north to south. First, on the east side: Henry and Margret Temperelli, John and Josie Giacomini, Severio ("Pepo") and Santina Galassi, Giuseppe and Chiara Rodolfi (Rudy's folks), Assunta Galassi, Joe and Lizzie Bedolli, Tom and Kat Mernin, Mrs. Delam Decamarte, Sesto and Kattie Paoni, and Tony & Mary Mitchell.

On the west side, north to south, again: "Campita" (a bachelor) and later George and Della Maurer, Legerra and Justinella Santogrossi, Louie "Skeets" and Florence "Tootsie" Galassi, Mr. and Mrs. Brooks Byus, Joe and Della Mordock, Mrs. Mordock, Joe and Liz Beja, and Constantino "Gusto" and Catarina Giacomini (Dominic's grandparents).

There was a skip or two in the above recitation because of unimproved lots, Rudy explained to me, as she caught her breath.

Donna Street and Mayden Avenue

Just for good measure, Rudy let fly with Center Street (Donna Street) residents too. Nancy and Jim Bartlett aided the recollection process since Jim lived on Donna most of his long life, as did Nancy. Starting on the east side of the street (south to north, this time): Mr. and Mrs. Bob Bartlett, Sr., Tony & Mrs. Bedolli, Richard and Helen Douglas, Mr. & Mrs. Linn, the Kush (or Kuss) brothers (bachelors), Felix (Toots) & Helen Sefick, Mrs. Emma Galassi, John (Miz) & Sophia Geyston, Mr. & Mrs. Quinnegan, and (on Randy Street) Bill & Ann Usaplet.

Going south to north on the west side of Donna Street were: Fofi's Market/Jailhouse Tavern, Tony & Eva Antonacci, Mr. & Virginia Kinzora, Domenic & Mrs. Giacomini (and later Ernie & Jennie Willis), Andy & Irene

Golesh, Mr. & Mrs. Sloper, (then two lots for baseball), Frank (Chops) & Stella Sefick, and two unmarried sisters.

Jim and Nancy, having fun with this recitation, then added families on the north side of Mayden Road, starting after Fofi's Market/Jailhouse Tavern, going west: Pasquale & Maria Fofi, John & Albina Paoni, Paul & Nunciata Paoni, Dolcito Mickeletti family, unknown, Sam & Frances LaFura, Mr. & Mrs. Sukalaski, and Nazzareno & Felicia Rondelli.

A couple of caveats: First, on the above streets there were left out several empty lots. Second, some of these families may have been mixed up time-wise, some since they represent a couple generations. For example, the Giacominis on Donna Street built their house which was later sold to Ernie & Jennie Willis.

Butcher Day – by Linda Mae Giacomini Gent

I don't know who wrote their life story first, Merino or Linda Mae. But both siblings did a fine job capturing those parts that opened Devereux's windows to that world. The following is a detailed yet succinct picture into an important day in the lives of immigrant Italians who lived in the early parts of the 20th century. I enjoyed Linda Mae's portrayal of how the Italian men slaughtered and then butchered a pig for the family's important food source and how the community pitched in. It is almost the exact same story my mother relays in my biography of her.

Dad went to a farmer as soon as possible in the spring. After a few months of feeding the pig, it was big enough to be called a hog. When the time came to butcher the hog, my dad called his best friend, Mr. Paoni, to help him. Mr. Paoni had a huge butcher knife that no one else was allowed to use. They helped each other every year.

They built a hanger [support] made of wood. After the hog was butchered it was hung on the hanger for four hours, just enough time for the workers to have a beer! Then it was time to cut the hog.

The first cut was the ham. It was cured with salt and pepper, then wrapped in heavy paper. For a long time, it hung in our basement. By spring, it was a delicious piece of cured meat.

The next piece was the 'lonza,' a little more delicate than the ham.

Then it was time to make sausage. First the meat was ground and then it was put into the casing. We had spent many days getting the intestines clean. The sausage was tied around a flat piece of wood to keep until summer. All this was put in the basement. The sausage was good after hanging in the basement, but I liked it more when it was fried with green dandelions that Mom and her friends picked in the farmer's ground.

The next thing was to render the lard. The skin was not used, only the fat. Making lard from fat was women's work. The fat was cut into pieces, then rendered and put into crocks. The crocks were put in the basement. By the next day, it was hard enough to use. Lard was not only used to fry, but it was used to make pie crusts. No one wanted butter to be used for pie crust.

Delivery Services

Rudy mentioned to me that not everybody was in the position to always afford butchering their own stock, or having enough meat and other food. At that point, she confessed, "We even, on occasion, had to take advantage of the 'relief wagon,' which was what passed for Public Aid assistance in those days. It would go around the village and provide needy families—and there were lots of us—with free sugar and flour and foodstuff like that."

She also told me about trucks that delivered fresh meat to houses. "The truck from Peters Market had meat in the back that was wrapped in white bed sheets. When it stopped at a customer's house, the driver would cut off a hunk of whatever she wanted."

People told me that in the old days their parents or grandparents would buy basic needs at Fofi's and then, if they needed more and when they could, walk down Sangamon Avenue, above the viaduct, and purchase other foods from Taposik's Grocery Store [sometime in the late 30's or early 40's].

Rudy said few people had transportation other than hoofing it. No cars in the early days. Some people had horse-drawn wagons, and that was rare too. "Dad was able to buy or barter an old white mare and cobble together a wooden buggy. That really helped us."

Summary

I love reading, talking, and writing about peoples' lives. Especially ordinary people. Each year I reread the classic play "Our Town" by American playwright Thornton Wilder. Most kids nowadays read it sometime in high school. It is also one of the most popular stage productions put on by high school drama clubs. It is simply a play that venerates the ordinary lives we all live but don't seem to appreciate until we are old or sick.

That's why I wanted to highlight the stories of the common folk who took up residence in Devereux Heights, which is about as ordinary a community as there is. Every one of the families who has ever lived there has remarkable stories to tell. And I love to bring them to light.

I was able to get to enough interviews from people who represent most of the decades, so you have a pretty good idea what things were like in much of the life of this vibrant hamlet. For those very early years, I tried to write down honest stories from my research phase.

I also interjected some stories from my own grandparents and my mother's early days in Starnes. I did this because where and how they lived in the early 20th century was very similar to how their kindred immigrants from Devereux lived since they were contemporaries. I hope I didn't put too much of me in it—my wife always reminds me, "Now, Ken, this is their story, not yours."

Devereux Height's Hero

Angelo "Judge" Galassi. 1908—1944
(Courtesy Joe Galassi.)

Chapter Seven

Personal Stories

I **n this chapter I will relate more stories of folks living in Devereux, but these will be more on the personal level.** They are about challenges, overcomings, and other intimate situations they had experienced in their lives.

A True Hero

There may be several people who came out of the rich traditions of Devereux Heights who may be called genuine heroes in the best sense of the word. But there is none more fitting to be called a true hero than Angelo Galassi, one of its native sons. His nickname was "Judge." (I also heard others refer to him as "Shorty.")

PFC Galassi was killed in action in Normandy, France, just a few days after the D-Day Invasion that occurred on June 6, 1944. After surviving the horrific landing, Angelo, age 35, was killed while on a patrol on June 9. His parents were Louis and Emma Galassi.

His obituary in the *Illinois State Journal* on September 2, 1944, states that Galassi "was born on November 26, 1908, and attended local schools. Before entering service on Feb 7, 1942 he was employed at Herndon's Construction Co. He received preliminary training at Ft. Lewis, Wash., and at army camps in California and Maryland before being sent overseas. He was survived by four brothers, five sisters and his mother."

I asked several people in Devereux what Angelo was like. Most said the obvious things like he was a great guy, a nice guy. But his nephew, Jim Galassi, told me he idolized him. Here was his take on his beloved uncle, whose picture (along with his other uncles in the military) hangs proudly in his and his mother's home on Angelo Street:

He was a tough, tough kid growing up, I heard. He actually carried two pistols on him sometimes. I was shocked when I heard the news. I thought to myself, "Nobody could kill 'Judge'. It's not possible."

Dominic Giacomini told me that, "My dad always mentioned his dear friend, "'Judge,' who was a hero in World War II."

Judge was honored when his sister, Helen Sefick, made sure the Italian street was memorialized as Angelo Street. He is also honored by being buried among the other thousands of Americans interred in the American Cemetery in Normandy, France.

Circumstances or Divine Guidance?—by Rudy Rodolfi

Rudy is one of the most famous of Devereux Heights' sons and daughters. She made her mark on the softball diamond after high school. (Remember there were no girls' sports in school, except for GAA, until Title IX passed in 1969.) Rudy discovered she had a real affinity and love for the game. She played for a number of teams during her 18-year amateur career: Salvation Army, Madison Furniture, the Caterpillar Diestlettes, Sunnyland-ettes, and Pekin-ettes. Playing excellent ball (mainly as a catcher) qualified her as a member of the Springfield Sports Hall of Fame.

Many don't know Rudy had the opportunity to play baseball for the Rockford Peaches in the All-American Girls Professional Baseball League (AAGPBL) during the war years, but turned it down since she needed to hold on to her job with Caterpillar in Peoria, where she worked her entire career. That team and that league were featured in the 1992 movie "A League of Their Own."

Here is the poignant drama that played out in her family's life before she was born, in her own words.

My dad, Giuseppe Rodolfi, came to America from Gubbio, in central Italy, sometime before 1907 and settled south of Williamsville, Illinois, two miles [in a tiny burg called Selbytown, near a mine]. *He lived as a boarder for some time with a friend from the Old Country, Joe Damiani, along with his wife Assunta. The couple had four children, but Dad soon found out Assunta was dying from the 1918 Spanish Flu. She was concerned about her children and husband, and so wrote her sister, Clara, back in Italy, to come to America and marry Joe.*

A week after Assunta passed, Joe also came down with influenza that following January, and, like so many young people, he also died. While on his death bed, Joe asked Dad to take care of his children. Dad immediately wrote Clara and told her of the double catastrophe and begged her to marry him, based on Joe's wishes. She agreed, however, due to a snafu with immigration, it was not until the next August that she would be in Springfield. In the meantime, Dad enlisted families to take care of the kids until Clara arrived.

Several months later, on August 16, 1919, Clara made the two-week voyage, arriving in Springfield to meet my dad at a pre-arranged spot, DiCenso's Grocery Store located downtown [at 810 E. Washington]. It was by chance that Clara happened to see her brother, Adolfo, walking down the street when she was taking a cab to the store. She excitedly stopped the cab and waved her brother down. Adolfo brought his sister the rest of the way to meet Giuseppe.

My dad married Clara, as agreed, on August 25, 1919. They decided to move to Devereux and raise the kids there.

Dad and Clara, eventually my mother, had five of their own children. So, Mom was raising eight kids all together—one of the stepchildren had died. Dad never adopted Joe's children because he wanted them to keep their own surname, Damiani, as he promised his friend he would do.

Around 1925, Mom was feeling homesick and wanted to return with all the children to Italy. I felt Mom was not thinking rationally at the time due to some personal circumstances. (This was before I was born, in 1928; I was the last child Mom had.) She eventually came to her senses and decided against the move. She and Dad stayed in the same house in Devereux the rest of their lives.

Dad was a quiet, thoughtful man. He was very smart and a real philosopher about understanding people. He would not argue, but he loved to sing.

I always remember the advice he gave all of his own children as we grew up: "You must understand about your other brothers and sisters and their background, because you haven't lost anything. They lost their real parents; therefore, they will have first choice over you." We all respected that strong feeling on his part. And they always did get first choice, and it never bothered us.

The Dreaded Whistle

Everybody in a mining community is keenly aware of what it means when the mine whistle blows: Trouble. Big trouble. Everyone stops what they are doing, and they start heading to the mine. It's due to one of the three unmentionables: a cave-in, a bad accident, or an explosion. Janassio (Geno or Gene) Giacomini, only 28 and with a family, was involved in a deadly accident at Peabody #59 (AKA Jones & Adams), just a mile's walk from the village. It occurred on Friday, April 2, 1943. Rudy never forgot that terrible day: "I was just a young girl but remembered the incident." Apparently, Gene and another miner were unloading coal from a "car " (i.e., wagon) on an elevated rail into a railroad hopper. Somehow it began to flip over— maybe the weight distribution was off kilter—and they both jumped off. Unfortunately, Giacomini landed on the exact spot where the wagon and coal ended up—on top of him. It was the only fatal accident I heard of that occurred to any Devereux miner. Here's a copy of the obituary in the *Springfield State Journal* dated April 3, 1943:

Gene Giacomini Dies Of Injuries

Miner Accident Victim In Peabody Pit.

Gene Giacomini, 28, of R. R. 5, died at 1:27 p. m. yesterday at Springfield hospital from arm and head injuries sustained in an accident at Peabody mine No. 59, Thursday. Coroner W. L. Dragoo will hold an inquest.

Surviving are his wife, Jane; daughter, Barbara Ann; son, Thomas J., all of city; father, Joseph; brother, Louis; two sisters, Miss Marie and Mrs. Zena Clemtine, all of Italy. He was a member of St. Aloysius parish.

Remains were removed to the Kirlin & Egan funeral home. Funeral arrangements are incomplete.

Luncheon Today To End Prayer Institute

A luncheon at 12:15 p. m. today in the Leland hotel at which a group of church workers will meet Dr. Glenn Clark and Glenn Harding, will conclude the prayer institute at the First Methodist church.

Doctor Clark's final address last night was "Prayer In an Age of Crisis." Harding led the opening song service and spoke on "Prayer as a Seed."

Daily Life in the Patch–by Merino Giacomini

This memoir piece from Merino Giacomini's autobiography will give you some idea what it was like living in Devereux during the early days, in the 1920s. Merino's parents, Constantino and Catherine Giacomini, were born in the small village of Purello, Italy, not far from Assisi which St. Francis made famous. Constantino came to America in 1900 at age 13 and worked alongside his father in the coal mines of southern Illinois. He went back to Italy to marry and returned with his Catherine in 1907.

The young family heard that the mines in central Illinois were safer and moved to Devereux, where Constantino secured a job at the Chicago-Springfield Mine. They then began their family, eventually having seven children. Merino was the last child, born in 1924. They purchased a house on Angelo Street.

During the late part of the summer months and early fall, Dad's vegetable garden and fruit orchard would yield an abundant amount of food. Mom would round up all the empty jars she could find and would then start canning all of the fruits and vegetables that Dad could possibly harvest.

There were times when she would exhaust her supply of jars and she would borrow more from her friends, or if money was available, she would purchase more of them to add to her collection. Even after using up all that she had, there was always extra fruits and vegetables left over. Being a very frugal person, Mom hated to waste anything, so any leftovers would be fed to the flock of chickens that she would invariably keep.

I can still picture her going into the chicken house and gathering up the eggs. There was an apron that was constantly tied around her waist. She would pull up the two bottom corners to form a bowl-like place to put the eggs in. She would always have a few kind words for the chickens, especially if their production met her expectations. She dearly loved those chickens.

As if Mom didn't have enough to do, she and Dad decided to take in some boarders to add to their income. They ended up with 11 of them, all big husky, and seemingly always hungry, coal miners.

Later in her life she would frequently reminisce about those long hard days. She would mention about how she would get up early every morning to prepare eleven lunch buckets for the boarders, plus one for Dad. Those "buckets" didn't consist of a finger sandwich and an apple. They were filled with enough food to satisfy a small horse. The bottom part of the miner's bucket was a separate compartment that held about a gallon of water. That section had to be washed and filled with clean water. This was before indoor plumbing invaded their home, which meant that the water had to come from the well that was situated about 30 feet from the house. There would be times during those winter mornings when it would get so cold one's hands would stick to the freezing pump handle.

Every other day Mom would bake twelve or more loaves of bread, that those big hungry miners would speedily consume. She would say that they were reminiscent of hordes of termites polishing off a two-story house. She would talk about how every Monday morning she would have to wash mountains of clothes, clothes that were drenched with sweat and coal dust. In addition to all of the above, she still managed to cater to the needs of her children. As I write this, I can't help but wonder, in amazement, how she lived through all that. It wasn't only hard work; it was also the hardships that she and Dad had to endure through those years.

186

The only means of transportation in those days was done afoot. They didn't have the luxury of a horse or automobile. They had to walk a long way for groceries and other needs. Most of their neighbors faced the same dilemma.

One very cold winter night, the roads were covered with snow and ice, making it almost impossible to walk on them. My youngest sister Lena picked such a night to become very sick. Mom and Dad didn't know what was really wrong with her but they both knew that something had to be done. The nearest doctor was well over three miles away.

My dad was always blessed with a certain amount of ingenuity. He was aware of the fact that walking on ice for that distance was not going to be a simple task, so he went down the basement, found an old pair of shoes and drove nails through the soles from the inside with the points sticking through the bottom. Thus solving the problem of slipping on the ice and probably hurting himself or Lena. My sister was bundled up and Dad carried her the three plus miles to the doctor's house with the snow and ice pelting his face all the way.

Avoiding Fascism –by Linda Mae Giacomini

In her autobiography, *Memories and Poems of Linda Mae Giacomini Gent*, the Merino's sister begins her story as an eight-year-old girl preparing to move from Devereux to Purello, Italy, where her parents were from.

She is sad because Italy seemed a "distant place," and she did not understand the reason for uprooting her three sisters and brother—plus herself. After all, she had only known America. Her father, Constantino, wanted to be near his father, Leopolo, and spend some time with him before he died. He had come to America with his dad when he was 13 years old, and they worked side by side in the coal mines. In 1921, at age 20, he returned to Italy with his father only to marry his girlfriend. The young couple came to America and ended up in Devereux, eventually with four children. (One child, Merico, had died while they lived in a mining town in southern Illinois.) Life was good for several years, and then her father began thinking about going back to Italy.

Dad was anxious to see his father before he died and soon it was all settled. We were going to leave Devereaux and live in Italy permanently. My mother was not too happy because she had saved some money to buy a small grocery store [DiCenso's Italian-American Store]. In those days, the men were the head of the house.

Her father had been sending money every week with instructions to a builder in Purello for their new house. By her account, it was quite the place, a five-story structure to take care of all the family's needs. The first floor was for the oxen. The second floor was for the kitchen. The third floor was the bedroom for the four children, with a thin wall between the boy and the girls. The fourth floor was a "commissary" to keep vegetables and fresh fruit. The top floor was for a toilet ("il gabinetto"). My guess is that it was a palace compared to the other homes in the town.

When my Aunt Santina, my father's sister, knew for sure we were going to Italy, she decided I should live with her and her husband. His name was Pepo. Of course, the answer [from her parents] was 'no.' Had I known my parents would return to Devereaux so soon, I probably would have stayed with Aunt Santini [sic], Only one thing would have kept me there. She had a popcorn popper with a basket. We were still using a skillet on top of the stove.

Once in Italy, little Linda Mae recounts her first impressions:

I can never forget the rumbling of the train from Cherbourg [France] to Purello. Some of the seats were velvet but some felt like we were sitting on boxes. I can still remember after riding miles and miles, the conductor gave us a chance to get off the train with the words, "Get back in time!"

We were very happy to be allowed to touch the one tree with olives and the other with figs. I do not remember if we were allowed to eat the fruit.

Grandpa and Grandma were waiting for us for dinner and there was a bedroom waiting for us for the night. We were practically starved. I think things were scarce. They told us they wanted to give us spaghetti, but all she could come up with was bread and wine. In my mind, I can still see her standing near the wooden box where she kept her bread, homemade, of course.

The rest of the story gives the reason why food—and everything else—was hard to come by. After a few months getting adjusted to their new home and life in Italy, entering school, etc., Constantino noticed some unsettling activities. Fascista began holding meetings in the local church and there was talk of war. Her brother was at the beginning age to be drafted for the army.

Because of World War II, my dad wanted to be in America before the war broke out. We returned to America . . . . My dad came back alone six months before the rest of us. He was eager to find us a house in Devereaux since we had sold our house to a family named Rodolfi.

Dominic Giacomini added to this story of his aunt's after reading the draft form. These are his words:

Constatino, Linda May's father, was my grandfather. He was a very wise man. Even though he never finished grade school, he was to me like a very educated person. (And I have his name as my middle name.) He once explained his sudden decision to quickly move back to the United States: "We are returning to America because I can see war coming soon and I don't want my son fighting against my beloved country, America!" That son he was referring to was my father.

This story reminds me that most all the men and women who immigrated from the Old Country—in this case Italy—were not interested in returning back home. My grandparents emphatically told me, "Why go back—there's nothing there."

Rudy's father responded just as simply: "Are you crazy? Why would I want to go back again? It's just rocks and hills and hunger."

The First Black Family in the Village— by Brad Mills

Several people suggested I call up and meet with Brad Mills. When I asked why, they said he was well connected, knew a lot about Devereux, and was very personable. In addition, Brad had been trying to pull together a North-End association from the three close communities— Indian Hills, Devereux and Twin Lakes.

We had something in common because he is a first cousin of Peter Lou, my old St. Al's schoolmate. He corrected me that Pete was not technically from Devereux, that he grew up just west, across the tracks. "My mom and Pete's mom are sisters."

Brad is African-American and told me the story when he and his family moved into the village. Others I've interviewed told me the same story, but this is from Brad himself.

Mom and Dad lived on the south side of Springfield and decided to move north, so they chose Devereux. In 1963, we bought a house on Piper Road, just three houses north of Neil Street. It was a nice place, and it was easily affordable since both Mom and Dad worked. Well, when he first saw us moving in, our next-door neighbor freaked out. He wasted no time putting up a ten-foot *wooden fence between us. The funny thing was that other neighbors saw him as being close-minded and told him so. Except for this fellow, the whole village was very accepting of us, and I've made my home here ever since.* [He now lives in the very house of that neighbor who put up the fence! How's that for poetic justice?]

When I asked if they were the first black family to live in the village, he thought there might have been at least one other, but he wasn't sure. (Other people told me the Mills were the first.)

The one point he emphasized over and over was a common refrain from most all my interviewees: Devereux is one of the most friendly, community-minded places you could ever hope to find. He went on in that vein:

The town was, and still is, tight, I can tell you that. Everybody knew everybody else and what they were up too. No secrets. It was safe too. Everybody looked out for everyone else. As an example, if some teenager was having a problem with a girlfriend or boyfriend, a concerned person—it wouldn't necessarily be a neighbor—might sit down with the youngster and listen them out. You know, be supportive. That's just how things were and still are here.

On the other hand, if you weren't from Devereux and wanted trouble, you'd get all the trouble you'd want. That's for sure. Tight knit, that's for sure. And it's still like that.

How Immigrants Were Viewed by Some

The Letter to the Editor I mentioned twice in Chapter Four, where that person rants against the (mostly) immigrants of Devereux, should give us pause at how new arrivals were looked upon and treated by some Americans during the various waves of immigration. Since I am half Italian, I have heard many of those stories from my grandparents and other relatives. I think it may be instructive to quote some more from that prejudiced critic to give you an understanding of what most of the Devereux people had to endure from many (but certainly not all) more established citizens of Springfield. I place this under the "personal stories" because that stark attitude was as personal at it gets.

Out on the northeast part of town is a settlement of foreigners. The people there are un-American in every way. Scarcely any of the women understand English, and the men know very little of the language of this country except the oaths and orders of their employers. They live in nice clean cottages—that is, the cottages are nice and clean upstairs, but the people, almost without exception, live in damp, dirty cellars with the poultry and pigs. They simply feel more at home in the cellar, they haven't gotten use to American houses. The men work in the mines, around about, or the zinc works . . .

. . . The majority of the women of the little settlement are hopelessly ignorant. Mrs. John Caldwell tells of the crippled children who are brought from Pryor [School] to St. John's hospital to the Children's Clinic. Children whose pitiful condition was caused by the ignorance of the parents, children who have never sat up, children who have never spoken. One little boy last week, from Pryor school district, was brought to Dr. East's clinic. He was seven years old and

has never talked—they said he was deaf and dumb and idiotic. Dr. East took a dime from his pocket and held it out towards him. "You can have this sonny, if you reach for it," he said. Needless to say, the little fist reached out for the money, proving that his brains were all right, that it was just the neglect or ignorance of his parents which had resulted in his apparent stupidity . . .

. . . Mrs. J.S. Hanes canvassed the district Monday, from 10:00 a.m. until 3:30 p.m., trying to get the women to register for patriotic service. She took with her an interpreter, a young woman who could speak four languages. In that time, she could find only two women who could speak English. One Polish woman was totally ignorant of the fact that America was in the great war. She told Mrs. Hanes, through the interpreter, that she was glad the war was over, so that she could return to her own country. She folded her arms tightly across her bosom and sunk her head between her shoulders, as though the thought of America chilled her very soul, and wailed, "God, I want to go home. . . ."

. . . Another woman refused to register—"no," she told the interpreter, "I won't have anything to do with you.

You ask my name, you go away, pretty soon you come back with bill to pay." They were all suspicious and afraid—What has been done to these poor foreigners to make them live in terror of Americans?

There, at the very gate of Springfield, this prosperous, thriving, smug old town, lies misery, ignorance and a helpless people. Springfield men and women go about their own affairs—is it Just careless neglect, or pure selfishness?

The committee on women and children in industry . . . is working with the School Club Council to do what is possible toward the Americanization of the community, which has been set down boldly in our midst from the plains of "Little Russia."

Another Kind of War Casualty— by Rudy Rodolfi

On my second visit to Rudy's home on Upper Peoria Lake (where the river is a mile wide behind her house), she casually mentioned her brother in relation to the story that Merino Giacomini told about the town character, "Joe," mentioned above. She had read through the first draft of my book and exclaimed, "He may have been talking about my brother, 'Crax.' He was the oldest brother of my actual

197

siblings. He was born in May of 1920." She continued, "The only thing is, he was not a whiskey drinker, like in that part where he pours it in that watermelon half. But he did wear bibs all the time and he did have a car." When I asked her to tell me more, she opened her heart and shared a sweet and tragic story I felt should be included in this chapter about life in the village.

His name was Joe Freddie, but we called him Crax because he loved soda crackers and was always eating them. You asked me what he did for a living. That's a good question. He was a poor student, got held back and graduated with two of our siblings from 8th grade. He was 16.

He got a job at Ford Hopkins Drug Store downtown in Springfield. He wasn't there too long because he left for his physical in Rockford on December 10, 1941—just three days after Pearl Harbor. We didn't see him again until May of 1946.

He came back, as so many did, a changed person. He was in the medical corps and apparently saw some bad stuff. He was in Karachi, India [now Pakistan] and also saw action around the Burma Road. He was a shy and backward kid and, I suppose, couldn't handle it. (In one letter to me he wrote, "They would have me hand out medicines to the fellows. But sometimes, I would run and hide: I couldn't stand seeing them like they were.") He got to drinking over there and once home he continued drinking. He drank until he died.

I was working at Caterpillar, and I came home from Peoria every weekend on the Interurban to help Mom and Dad. I would have to go down by the Stockyards at the Mighty Fine Inn tavern to get him. I did that almost every weekend. It broke my folks' hearts.

Before the war he was a better athlete than us girls. I remember, could he run. He'd go down by the Interurban and run laps—all the way down from Mayden to the Bypass and back again. He'd do that over and over.

Poor Crax was never sober after he came back. He drank mainly beer. My family tried to help him by getting him jobs to take his mind off of drinking. My sister Olga lived on a farm and brought him out there as a farm hand. She couldn't get him to work. My brother Geno took him on construction, telling us, "I'll sober him up." That didn't work. Then, my sister Freda, who was in Detroit with her husband, tried. He worked as a tile setter and got him to work with him and that didn't work. My sis Rita's husband worked at the Motherhouse in Riverton. He got him on there, driving the nuns around, cleaning, taking care of the yards, that kind of stuff. Nothing worked.

Then, Dad died and later Mom died, and their house was left to my sister Mary and me. We had Crax live with Mary—he never married and neither did she. Mary and I remodeled the house and really fixed it up. Crax didn't help at all; he just kept drinking. He couldn't hold a job. When I'd come home for the weekends, Mary would be mad because she locked the door when she went to bed and Crax would come home late and be irate, hollering and banging on the door.

One time during the week he called me and said, "Nora (what my family and friends called me), you got to do something about Mary, she's driving me crazy! It can't go on like this! I'm going to kill her. If she keeps locking the door at night I'm is going to just burn the house down." That's when I decided we needed to get Mary and him out of the house.

We eventually sold the house and Mary moved to Grandview. We had had plans when we retired to have all three of us living together—we three who never got married. Instead, I bought him a trailer and he lived in that trailer court just past the tracks as you leave Grandview.

As we got older, Mary and I decided to change our wills to take into account how we could distribute our assets to our nieces and nephews. I called Rosco Bongean, an old Italian lawyer everybody in Devereaux used, on a Saturday morning to go see him. But Mary died in the backyard of her house that same morning when I went over to get her.

Since I got Mary's money in the will, I divided it all and gave $600 to each of our nieces and nephews—all 21 of 'em. I kept Mary's house for a year and then sold it. I sold it to my niece Diane Silveri for one dollar.

In the meantime, Crax was still drinking and working sporadically. He worked when he absolutely had to but basically lived on the largesse of family members, including me. But it so happened that a couple barflies that he hung around with took pity on him and helped him out too. They actually looked out for him.

He soon after that died at 75 of cirrhosis of the liver. He didn't have a will, so I couldn't get into his bank accounts (He had two, to my surprise) to pay for his funeral. I went to Bisch Funeral Home. (Bisch had buried all four of my siblings for nothing, can you believe that?) I didn't know what to do, so I told Mr. Bisch's grandson and he concocted a plan. He said he would make out a larger bill for the funeral service and to take it to the first bank and hand them the bill. Then come back and I'll give you the difference. He said to do the same with the second bank.

I had $500 left over after those two transactions and Bisch got paid for his services. Wasn't that kind of him? I gave that money to Olga who was living off of Sangamon Avenue and Henley. We buried my brother at Camp Butler Military Cemetery down by Riverton, and I gave his trailer to a lady friend of his.

Those two women he drank with really took care of him. They got him his military pension and put most of the money in those two bank accounts for him. You sure can never tell people by what they seem. Those barflies were his angels, when you think about it.

That nice boy was ruined by the war. He came back different. He was never the same. I sure hope he was that "Joe" that Merino was talking about. If he was, he did some good with his life after all.

He did good by his family too. The one thing I can say about my brother was that he was what they call "a good ole boy." Everybody loved Crax, especially our nieces and nephews. He taught most of them how to drive. And he was a great babysitter for them. He had this shining personality and he could tell whoppers all day long that sure sounded like the truth. Few people had any idea of the inside story; maybe that's the way it should be. Maybe there was a little good in him. We all loved him.

One of Crax nieces, Judy (Handley) Hawks also told me, while talking at a local Panera, that their affable uncle would often give them rides to school. He certainly made many positive impacts on lots of lives.

The Giacomini brothers playing bocce ball, like the old days in Devereux. Merino & Domenic, around 2007. (Courtesy Dominic Giacomini)

Chapter Eight

The Village Today

The story of Devereux Heights continues to this day. The original little village is not much larger than planned by Harry Devereux in 1913, when the lots started to be sold. Several generations have grown up there and carried on their families' names. What follows are some significant events that have occurred in the last couple of generations.

Finally, Neighbors

Two subdivisions sprang up near Devereux to more than triple the population of the area. Gail M. Wanless developed Indian Hills in the 1950s, just southwest of Devereux and continued into the next decade to form a thriving middle class community. (It lies just across Sangamon Avenue from St. Aloysius church.)

Also, Devereux's sister village of Twin Lakes was also put in by the Barker-Lubin company. That community, southeast of, and contiguous with, Devereux, added another several hundred people in the middle '60s and early '70s and '80s. Its name gives away the fact that its central feature are two lakes whose basin formed the beginning of the draw that becomes the ravine through Devereux. That addition was essentially the Simko farm discussed before. (Barker-Lubin also acquired the small, 15-acre Mayden farm and built homes on it.)

Thus, Devereux is no longer an isolated island with little connection with other close-by communities. The former enclave is now part of an active little opolis with two neighboring communities. But due to geography, history and communal spirit, it retains its identity and values.

A few years back Brad Mills spent a lot of time and energy trying to bring all three communities into the fold of what I would quip a North-North-End Neighborhood Association. There was opposition to it by a few people, but enough so his efforts never achieved full traction. That's too bad in a sense, but group identity is a strong force, and I suppose that's like the difficulty with small, rural unit schools not wanting to consolidate. It's all about loyalty and identity. (I saw that up front and personal when I lived in Mason City, Illinois.) Still, these three close neighbors are friends and cooperate when area issues come before them.

When I asked him if he tried to organize an association of just Devereux people, he said it would be a great thing, but he had been burned out trying to get all three united and may attempt this limited plan in the future. Hopefully, this will happen because this village started it all and deserves its own recognition and continued cooperation among its people as well as its neighbors. Maybe in some small way this book will ignite that interest.

Indian Hills, a local resident told me, has had a couple of loose neighborhood associations, although I could not find a website dedicated to either one of them. There are two major garage sales each year, at which time there is a coming together of the community, I was told. Someone else mentioned an active Neighborhood Watch group as well.

Twin Lakes, however, appears from its comprehensive and well laid-out website to have a thriving association with an informal government of sorts and lots of associated activities, such as the Big Fireworks Display on each Fourth of July. One board member said they heard their neighborhood association was the largest and strongest of any in the city of Springfield.

If I could throw my two cents into this, I would suggest Devereux residents harken back to the past and allude to the fact that their village began as a company mining town and consider giving themselves the name "Devereux Diggers." This recognition of mining might be one contributing factor that gives it the identity their village deserves. Had they had a school of their own, that nickname would have been an appropriate school mascot name. Just an idea.

Population Figures

I took an estimate of the populations of this cluster of communities. Devereux's population that I came up with is based on a rough count of the number of residences, thanks to Google Maps. North Devereux or "Old Devereux" (everything north of Mayden Street) has 75 lots based on the old plat. If you take into account East Street doubling when its alley became Angelo Street and some lots being subdivided further through land transfers, plus other reasons, there might be 100 lots and houses.

South Devereux ("New Devereux")—most of which was developed by John H. Piper—can be considered the newer addition, with some larger lots and more contemporary homes. (Bob Yoggerst observed that "in the '60s there began a change-over of generations, who had more income to build nice homes in the area.")

That Piper Addition section has around 133 houses on its lots. If you add in the row of houses on Hedge Lane Road, you have another 18 residences. Assuming around four people per house, then the whole Devereux area might have 1000 souls nowadays, 400 in North Devereux and 600 in South Devereux.

The Indian Hills community has 990 people today, according to a website related to real estate sales. Twin Lakes has approximately 375 residences (based on garbage stops), which would equal around 1500 people.

So that area northeast of Sangamon Avenue has a combined population of perhaps 3500—a decent number to form an influential voting bloc or association group.

Houses For Sale?—Not Many

The day he went with me to interview his mother, Florence, at Sunny Acres Nursing Home, Jim Galassi brought to my attention something I had not thought about before: There is almost a total lack of FOR SALE signs in Devereux. (Bill Shay's home on an acre lot on Donna, together with out-buildings, is the lone exception at this time.)

He explained that "Devereux is so attractive as a place to live and raise a family that when somebody wants to sell, they put out the word and—presto—it's gobbled up fast." He went on that it's often relatives who want to stay close to other family members who buy the houses.

Two of the biggest selling points are seclusion and lot size. And, as I mentioned before, there is so much community pride that everybody takes care of their properties. After Jim educated me to that fact, I paid particular attention to the yards as I drove around the neighborhoods: I could see not even one yard that needed mowing. That's impressive.

Tearing Down the Village Walls

If you will recall in the chapter on Devereux businesses, "the local grocer and meat market owner," Jacob Kauth was one of the leaders in the movement for annexation of the village—just three years after it was platted. The 1916 article in the paper quoted Kauth:

Devereux Heights with the neighboring John H. Piper subdivision, forms one of the prettiest spots in the vicinity of Springfield. With the proper street improvements and conveniences installed, it could be made an exceptionally attractive suburb.

That prescient but premature sentiment was not pushed forward again for nearly 50 years. Following is the story behind what turned out to be a very contentious and controversial pathway from out-of-the-way place to full-fledged citizenhood for the village.

There had always been a water problem in the little village, according to some. Wells would be the first thing a new property owner would construct. It was strenuous work, digging wells by hand in the old days. Moreover, once you were at the 20 or 25 foot depth, you hit hardpan. It was tough digging through that stuff. Sometimes, the well diggers resorted to strongarm tactics, i.e., dynamite.

After all that work, water would sometimes be found to be bad—too much nitrate, or iron or even a foul smell— which would force owners to substitute cisterns for some of their fresh water needs. Other times, wells simply went dry. That was very good for Fred Flags's water hauling business. He was seen at all times of day and night driving around Devereux's streets in his water truck that contained a 1,000-gallon tank of fresh water for needy customers. Also coming to a head at this time was the rumor that Piper School's water source was   contaminated.

Another infrastructure problem was lack of sewer service in much of Devereux. Most everybody dug septic tanks with lateral fields. They work but sometimes plug up after several years of use. Residents on Piper Road were lucky: they had a sewer main since the Depression Era, it being installed with WPA funds and local labor.

Adding to those problems was that certain areas of town received more water during rainy seasons. In low lying areas, the high moisture in the soil would complicate the efficiency of the cisterns and septic tanks, not to mention flooding.

A final irritant was poor road maintenance by the county. One citizen told me the county maintenance crews would oil the streets in the summers and then leave piles of sand near each street for the residences to shovel it in front of their houses. Al Kenal, who wasn't interested in city help in any way, exclaimed there was a silver lining in that: "It was like other cooperative efforts: we all pitched in and spread the sand along our streets. It wasn't a big deal and we had fun doing it."

As the 1960s began, the quiet, grumbling voices of irritation and concern over water increased into a movement to bring Devereux into the City of Springfield and at last obtain then commonplace services: potable water, dependable road lighting, a comprehensive sewer system, and proper road maintenance. (Gas lines came to the village in 1960.) This cry was fueled by developer Barker-Lubin who represented the proposed new subdivision just across Mayden Avenue, to be christened "Twin Lakes." Naturally, it needed those infrastructure services as much as or more than its neighboring village.

The call for water, including the corresponding entry into the city, was a great push and pull, as you can imagine. The naysayers had good wells, didn't' want to have to hook onto the new sewers, didn't want increased taxes, and liked things "just the way they are." Devereux was like an island until itself and the conservative elements were content to stay disconnected, as it were.

As often happens in such matters, a strident champion of change appears on the scene to push progress ahead of tradition. In this case it was a small contingent of promoters led by Vince Galassi, who formed the Devereux Heights Water Organization (in 1964), of which he was president with six trustees. Laura told me her father, his son-in-law John Bensi and Teresa Mayden put in an extra $1000 apiece, in addition to their original contribution of the same amount, to convince the city they were serious about the $54,000 improvement price tag. (They were later reimbursed for their commitment, she said.) Vince then enlisted the efforts of Helen Sefick, Louis Mills, Curly Jones and a few others who wanted water and wanted it fast. His little cadre of true believers went door to door, leaving no stone unturned. Helen was among the most committed.

(As I stated in a previous chapter, Vince Galassi was not related to Helen Galassi Sefick. These are two separate Galassi families.)

Brad Mills summarized his take on the whole situation to me over coffee at the downtown Café Moxo. He said when Twin Lakes' developer Barker-Lubin joined forces with Galassi and Company, the project was all but assured. The new development would simply tie into Devereux's water main (coming up from Sangamon Avenue along Piper Road). This then caused a ruckus that almost landed the whole mess in court. But these strong promoters worked their magic and (most of) the community annexed into the city, receiving their water.

What's interesting about this period was that some citizens were up in arms about coming into the city, while others didn't think much about it. Henry Temperelli put it bluntly to Bob Yoggerst: "These crazy old people are worried about taxes. Look what we're paying for now and we don't have anything."

The annexation process was eventually won in a lawsuit at the Appellate Court, resulting in the great majority of lots annexed in a phased-in plan. The local newspaper described the final process in the November 29, 1967 announcement:

Attorney Richard Grummon, representing the petitioners, said the petition completes a voluntary annexation program started in 1964. About 110 tracts, representing 80 per cent of Devereux Heights, will have become annexed under the program with council acceptance of the petition.

A week later that paper stated the City Council accepted that final petition. It went on to explain the benefits to that community and to the city as well. The 10-inch water main would be extended to all the new water customers and eventually to those who had once balked at coming in.

The most vocal holdouts in the entire village seemed to be a father and son team of George and Al Kenal. ("We were Lithuanian and our actual name was spelled something like 'Kennutas,' but no family member is exactly sure. Mom was Italian.") Al explains their position this way:

Our point was that our homes [on Angelo Street] were on property too low for sewer, and our well was just fine. It's still fine, by the way. So we saw no advantage. The whole of Devereux Heights is in the city limits except our house here. We are in unincorporated Sangamon County, and we like it that way.

In point of fact, there were actually quite a few more property owners who chose to stay out and they are out to this day. I don't know if I got across the tremendous amount of infighting, even family against family, but the rancor that the annexation created was very fractious to the community. It was not a fun time to be a Devereuxite. That was the only time in its century-plus history that the villagers were not together.

Streets Get New Names

One mystery for me (and even some residents) was how most of the streets were named or renamed. It was solved when I chatted with folks about this annexation period. Most of the originally platted roads were also renamed during this time. Most people around town either did not know the original names of their streets or did not care; they just used "Rural Route 5" and their mailbox numbers.

Here's the real story behind the name changes. Locals tell me Vince Galassi had enough sway to convince the city, which requires street names (for emergency reasons, etc.), for him to name and, if he wanted, to rename some of the streets. So, it was a perfect time to make changes and Vince stepped up to the plate in typical "I-can-do" fashion.

South Street was now Mayden Avenue, because the Mayden property (in the past) had extended along it much of the length of the village. My guess it may have been called that on an informal basis even earlier.

Helen Sefick saw to it that East Street was changed to Angelo Street in honor of "Judge" Galassi, Helen's brother who died in WWII. There is still a vestige of the original East Street name on the very northeast corner of the village.

North Street was changed to Randy Street in favor of whom no one seems to know. Someone told me that Randy Street got its name way before the annexation period; but no one could tell me whom it was named after. One person heard it was named by the owners who purchased the Usaplet property at the north end of Donna Street.

Center Street was now Donna Street for Vince Galassi's middle daughter.

Vincent Street was named after his truly, Vince himself.

Ida Mae Lane, a short street off of North Piper Road, was named for Vince's apartment manager, Ida Mae Willet. As mentioned above, he had cleared his salvage yard in that little cul-de-sac area and built a six-plex apartment building at the end of the short lane.

There is a very short Magdalena Street, just off of what would be East Randy, named after Vince Galassi's sister.

I heard Neil Road was named after one of the attorneys Vince, "H", and the others used during their water investment project. But Laura told me it was actually named after a friend of his, Noah Neil.

I have yet to find how Willow Lane got its name. But Curtis Mann emailed me an idea, which has merit:

I think I have a suggestion for the origin of the street name "Willow Lane." While looking through the plat book I found out that a little subdivision called Willow Brook is located on the north and south side of Willow Lane at the intersection with Piper Road.

While getting this information from my interviews, I discovered (as I mentioned above) there is a "North Devereaux" and a "South Devereux." The north part covers the original 1913 platted settlement (which had only five roads: North, South, East, and Center, plus Interurban Avenue). The boundary for this informal distinction is Mayden Avenue. Most of the new building around the village has been on the village's "south side," which takes in the side streets off of Piper Road, all the way down to Neil. (Much of, if not most of, South Devereux was originally the Piper Addition.)

Hedge Lane Road, which turns south at the east end of Neil Road, probably fits more logically with Twin Lakes subdivision, since it skirts it at its south edge. Oldtimers tell me it used to be called Mine Lane since it was close to Peabody #59. They also tell me there were several houses on the west side of that road. I haven't been able to verify either assertion.

Buying a Railway

The old Chicago & Alton Railroad had long ago abandoned its freight line through Devereux Heights. It had eventually sold its entire railroad system to Union Pacific, which has still been hauling passengers through Springfield on its passenger railway next to the old exempt Interurban track.

Around 15 years ago, some observant person contacted Union Pacific and asked the company if it would consider selling the old freight line right-of-way crossing through Devereux. Word eventually got out that the UP would be interested in divesting itself of that small swath of property between Mayden Avenue and Dirksen Parkway, not much more than a quarter of mile of railbed. I suppose it didn't want the headaches attendant to abandoned lines—problems like maintenance, insurance and liability.

A lady on Angelo Street by the name of Donna Holliday heard about UP's interest in selling, through the grapevine that included two real estate agents. She had three lots next to each other that would be impacted by any sale, so she thought about buying it herself. A similar railway sale gone awry made her think even harder about purchasing the land.

There was a man in a nearby town, Donna had heard, who some years earlier had purchased a disused railroad bed similar to this one and converted it into a long trailer court, positioning mobile homes on either side of a narrow road he placed in the middle of the old line. The townspeople were not happy having what they considered to be an eyesore, but they could do nothing about it after the fact. Donna found this prospect unappealing, both in terms of aesthetics and property values. She didn't want something like that in her backyard, nor in Devereux.

Donna quickly moved into civic activist mode and sought advice from a local Realtor as how to buy the railbed. This agent introduced her to a lawyer friend who ran a Springfield title company. The lawyer contacted Union Pacific on Donna's behalf and was able to consummate the sale for her. He handled both the transfer contract and the title work.

Donna held on to the property, confident in the fact that she had saved Devereux (and herself) from anyone exploiting that 150-foot wide swath of land, like that trailer court owner did. Then one day while at the courthouse to check on another property her family owned elsewhere in Springfield, she noticed that the railbed property had a tax lien on it. How could that be, since her attorney had taken Donna's check for the price UP asked? (He had instructed her to make the check out to him personally and he would pay the grantor.)

Donna immediately hired a high-powered attorney in town who specialized in property law and instructed him to straighten the mess out. He researched the situation and determined that the title company lawyer had taken the purchase money for his own use, never paying UP. "I crossed my fingers that UP would realize what had happened and take mercy on me." Her new attorney explained the fraud to the railroad company and, in the end, it agreed to grant Donna clear title to the railbed.

Around that time the newspaper ran articles that the same title lawyer who swindled her was in big trouble for other similar malfeasance. He eventually was convicted and sentenced to jail.

Donna then set about a proposal of offering roadbed sections to any landowners who had lots contiguous with it. She had the property surveyed (no small task in that jungle of overgrowth) and hired a real estate agent to contact all the landowners to see who was interested. The agent explained to each prospect along the way that they could add on to their back yards with either an extra 75 feet or 150 feet.

At first she received little interest, but as time went on neighbors began taking her up on her offer. Her real estate agent contacted Bob and Mary Yoggerst and Charlie Bedolli to get the ball rolling. Only Charlie was interested at the time, and he purchased his section plus one south of him and two north of him, since those contiguous owners weren't interested. That gave him four sections which amounts to 1.4 acres. [What I am calling a section is an area 100 feet wide (i.e., a lot width) by 150 feet long (the width of the railroad right-of-way)].

Eventually, Bob and Mary bought the four sections south of Charlie's purchase, which included the city's right-of-way for the defunct Randy Street. Rose Henderson, Mary's sister, who lived north off of East Street, purchased her section, which added to family land north to the by-pass.

Donna also sold four other sections south of the Yoggersts' purchases. She retained the eight remaining sections, giving her 2.75 acres. She also retained a similar sized right-of-way that bounds the Bypass. Her south railbed property begins at Mayden Avenue, where the sewer pumping station has a short easement, on up to and including her lots.

Bob and Mary began cleaning up their newly acquired land. And as Bob explains, it has been no small task:

It was a mess. There were trees, big vines growing up the trees, brush and shrubs—tons of poison ivy—so you couldn't even walk through it. It has taken us years of work to clear this all up. Mary and I decided to clean it up and have spent several years getting it into the shape you see here now.

Bob and Mary have transformed that impenetrable forest into a beautiful private "lineal park," which environmentalists use as the term for abandoned city railways made into long urban parks. He used his powerful little utility tractor, an assortment of implements for it, plus shovels, rakes, chain saw and hoes, to help in the transformation. They seasonably add bark mulch to the side pathways and more inch rock to the main trail. The husband and wife gardening team has planted strategically-located flowers including lots of tiger lilies, which take on a life of their own, spreading their beauty around.

One interesting element to their meandering "park" is a small concrete bridge he built over the creek at 'the crossover point" as Bob calls it. Standing there, he pointed to the place where the railroad company had built a 50-foot long, 14-foot high wooden trestle to support the tracks as the railway crisscrossed the ravine at the creek on its way to the mine.

He explained that the track entered the ravine on the west side of the deep "V" at Mayden. About half way to the mine it switched sides to the east of the ravine—the crossover point. This allowed the train to position itself next to the tipple to more easily load the hopper cars with coal.

Down a little farther (going north), Bob pointed out where there had been a bridge across the ravine as part of the original North Street [Randy Street] alluded to in Chapter Two. There is no remnant of it anywhere, just like there is no reminder that the rail line ever existed there, except for some of the flat ground of the rail bed and, as Bob tells me, "a few spikes I find now and then."

Charlie Bedolli, another hard worker in retirement, has beautified his four-section "park" in a similarly spectacular manner as his friends and neighbors have. Rose has decided to leave her section up to nature's whims, which the flora and fauna dearly appreciate.

What Happened to Devereux Mine?

By the way, the land just north of Rose's home proper, approximately three acres, is where the mine tipple was located as well as the two large shafts and the accompanying buildings and sheds.

This winter when most of the trees have lost their leaves and the bushes are thinned out, I am going to walk that north area (with Rose's permission) and see if I can discover any remnants from that once-producing mine that spawned the village to its south. I doubt I will, but you never know.

Walking that area with Bob and Mary, they pointed out who owns what pieces of properties north of their place along that ravine. I was amazed to see how far down that bottomland lies. It must be 30 feet in places. Now I understand why Rose decided not to clear her sections.

One thing they asked me to make clear is that all those improved sections I just wrote about, both unimproved and improved, are private property, just as are the adjoining lots with homes on them.

Bob tells me there are lots of deer, coyotes, squirrel and rabbits having a grand old time all along that ravine. Donna even has a couple of alpacas and a llama on her two acres of sections she retained plus the only pond in the village.

In a village you can't sack or fight with someone, as you'll find yourself stuck beside them in the hairdresser's next morning. –Jilly Cooper

Mr. Devereux, in his later years This is the
only other picture I could find of him.
(Courtesy SVC)

Conclusion

You now have an idea—hopefully a very good idea—what Devereux Heights was like—and is like. You learned about it from the vantage point of the experts— mostly from the lips of the local folks themselves. It was their story to tell and they did it as well as anyone could.

Whenever I write, I commit to tell the story about people "with warts and all." I did that with my father in *Rabbit Row*. I did the same thing with *Sister Raphael*, about my mother. I also did it in my several personal memoirs. I have continued to do so with this book. I wanted to report the people and events as they actually were and how they lived and how they happened.

What resulted from that principle is for you to critique. I just hope you now have a better appreciation of this rare jewel of a community. Because it was a ways off the beaten path, it has retained much of its charm and values and atmosphere it had a century to develop.

What it lacked in amenities, such as library, meeting center, doctor and a park, Devereux Heights has made up in sheer love of community. I saw that exemplified in word and deed. Did it have its dark side too? Of course it did. Doesn't every town? I hope I covered those negative aspects as well. You can't have one without the other.

Some of the people you met in this book are the last generation who remembers the first generation in Devereux. So, we were touching their shared history just as it is disappearing.

Someone told me, "Ken, you got here just in time!" I think I did in the sense that the people I interviewed allowed me to write down what their grandparents and parents didn't have time to record.

What we tried to do—those villagers who told me their history and I as their scribe—is preserve their past to honor those who created it. And I think we did that pretty well; at least I hope so.

Afterword

After having spent several months researching Devereux Heights, visiting it close to 40 times, talking with dozens of its citizens (whom I could not help but become friends with), and writing close to 50,000 words in this, Devereux's own life's story, I have recently imagined a dream of sorts. If you will indulge me this wonderful fantasy, I will share it with you.

It is in the form of what I would like to observe as reality, say in a couple of years, as I return to the village I have become fond of. It comprises a montage of several connected visions I see on a balmy summer's day.

As I turn onto Piper Road and up that main connecting link with the village—there are two others—I am excited to return for the first time in a while. I turn left onto Neil Street and the KC building at the end of the block. I turn right onto West Street and notice that green expanse of its property, but on it now is an actual park whose name I can make out clearly on a prominent sign: "**Centennial Village Park**." The park's central feature is a memorial, a block sculpture ten feet tall dedicated to those pioneering mining families who settled this area over 100 years ago, with names like Harry H. Devereux and Vince "Judge" Galassi emblazoned on it. No village should be without a park and now Devereux and its people finally have one.

Later, I have it explained to me that the village elders worked out an arrangement with the K of C Council. I didn't ask for details; I just smiled with approval that people figure these things out when they want to.

I return to Neil Street the way I came. As I turn left onto Piper again, I notice a commemorative neighborhood sign like you see at other historical neighborhoods throughout Springfield and other communities. It was simple but inviting: "**Welcome to Devereux Heights**." In the middle was a phrase in quotes *The Little Village That Could*. (Where in the world did they come up with that tag?) Then, at the bottom, the sign proudly concludes, "**Founded in 1913**."

Up the street at the T, I turn right at old South Street, now Mayden Avenue, and find myself in front of the most recognizable landmark in the village: the combination tavern and apartment. I pull over when a plaque on the corner of the old brick building catches my eye. I walk up to it and instinctively rub my hand over the raised bronze letters, which read:

This Property Has Been Placed On the
National Register of Historic Places
By the United States Dept of Interior
THE OLD FOFI MARKET
1922

With that honored designation, the present day owner of the building (or the community as a whole) had renovated the structure where it seems to look younger, more proud of itself and its history serving the villagers all those years.

I finish my drive up and down all the rest of the streets in the village, thinking of those people who opened up to me about their memories and those of their ancestors who lived here.

On my way out, I stop at the home of my friend, Brad Mills, to get the scoop on these wonderful improvements. He tells me it all started when people read this very book you hold in your hands.

"It was surprisingly easy forming a neighborhood association now that we were embracing our village history. Everybody wants to be a part of this village in an organized, 'let's do things' sense. It's almost magical, Ken, this new interest in this place."

Over sugary lemonade, Brad continues: "The association got busy fast: it put up the welcome sign, applied for the NRHP designation, and then talked with the K of C, many of whose members live in Devereux, like me."

He then told me, "And, Ken, you won't believe this. It gets better: there are two events we started that many other towns and villages have had for years. We instituted the Spring Village 5K Memorial Run where participants walk, jog, or run the entirety of the village's fifteen roads for some good cause we choose every year. And each October, we celebrate our village again as The Village Fall Festival, with booths and games and such. It kicks off with a typical parade beginning at what we call 'the village building' —Fofi's Market/Jailhouse Tavern—and ending at the park. Kids love it, and we even have street banners, floats and local personalities. It's a big affair."

I say goodbye to Brad and drive out onto Sangamon Avenue and then home, thinking, *Maybe the book was a good thing after all.*

Acknowledgements

The nature of this unfolding story of Devereux Heights required the input of local people who remembered some of the old days or recalled their parents or friends or neighbors talking about those now lost times.

The following are most of those contacts I made during my research phase. They were usually made through personal, eye to eye interviews, with me taking notes. I owe each of them a debt of gratitude for their time, memories and pictures. (I apologize if I left a name or two out.)

Dominic Giacomini, Barb McMeans, Diana Silvari, Judy Hawks, Rudy Rodolfi, Bob and Mary Yoggerst, Al & Karen Kenal, Jim & Nancy Bartlett, Brad Mills, Tom Blasko, Charlie Bedolli, Jim "Spibs" Galassi, Florence "Tootsie" Galassi, Donna Holliday, Bill Shay, Gladys Sefick, The Galassi Sisters—Barb, Donna and Laura Galassi, Pam Meyers-Jerome, Lou Menendez, Loren Martin, and Gene Weyant.

I owe a special thank you to Dominic Giacomini for suggesting writing about Devereux and then motivating me on to the finish line. (Several of his phone calls began with, "How are you coming along with the book?") He was my first contact three years ago, when he invited me to his house on the lake to discuss my book on the history of the North End of Springfield. During our pleasant chat, he showed me a copy of his uncle and aunt's memoirs about his growing up in Devereux in the early years. (He was kind enough to make me copies of them.)

Some village natives who were kind enough to review my draft manuscripts and correct dates, events, and especially all those (mostly) Italian names I butchered: Dominic, Rudy, Bob & Mary, Jim & Nancy, and Brad Mills.

Those who took out the time to review my manuscript to pen blurbs of nice comments: James Krohe, Jr., Mark McDonald, Curtis Mann, Virginia Scott, Brad Mills, Dominick Giacomini, Joe Giacomini, Bob & Mary Yoggerst, Jim & Nancy Bartlett, Taylor Pensoneau, Vickie Whitaker, and Springfield's mayor, the Honorable Jim Langfelder.

My editorial staff seems always to be spearheaded by my friend Virginia Scott, who has a way to make phrases and sentences sound better. She somehow is able to boil down wordy paragraphs to their essence. I depend also on my sweet and beautiful wife, Karen Kelly, to find those pesky typos and grammatical failings of mine.

I have relied on my boyhood friend and next door neighbor, Jerry Tansky, to copyedit most of my books, and he had agreed to bring his skills to this one as well. Thank you, Jerry, for a keen eye in the process.

An enormous thank you to two people who shared very personal stories about their families. Rudy Rodolfi gave me permission to place her stories about her family and brother. Joe Giacomini kindly allowed me to reprint some episodes from his father and aunt's memoirs. Those intimate entries added much in giving the reader insight into what life was like in those days in immigrant families.

Joseph Zeibert, senior planner for the Springfield Sangamon County Regional Planning Commission, was very helpful in providing various maps of the Devereux area, on his neat computer application that shifts from time period to time period. The several ladies across the hall at the

Sangamon County Recorder's Office spent time showing me how to retrieve land transfer records off the computer.

Thanks to Candice Cummins for providing rare pictures of people and scenes from Devereux and some of its citizens.

Randy Jones of IDOT's Mapping & Information Systems Unit also was a big help with maps. Dan Wheeler of Office of Mines and Minerals' Land Reclamation Division and Cheri Chenoweth of the Illinois State Geological Survey helped me with information and maps of the Devereux Mine.

I am so pleased that Mark McDonald saw value enough in the little village to devote a PBS TV program of "Illinois Stories by Mark McDonald" to it. I also want to thank the local folks he interviewed on the program: The Bartletts, the Yoggersts, Rudy Rodolfi, Al Kenal and Charlie Bedolli. And to Pam Meyers-Jerome for allowing us to tape the show in her tavern and to her son Michael who took pictures for me.

Finally, a big thank you to Curtis Mann and Stephanie Martin at the Sangamon Valley Collection at the Springfield Lincoln Library who responded willingly to my many requests for help in looking up people, places, maps, newspaper articles, and events about Devereux.

240

Appendix

Several Original or Close to Original

Devereux Heights Families

Bedolli

Joseph & Elizabeth. He came from Ancona, Italy. She was born in Illinois. He was a coal miner, she was a homemaker. They had 7 children: John, Fred, Pauline, Charles, Anthony and Albert. (Courtesy St. Aloysius Parish Cookbook, 1928—2003)

Galassi

Louis & Assunta (Marconi). He came from Gubbio, Italy; she from Peruggia, Italy. He was a coal miner and she was a homemaker. They had 10 children: Joseph, Theodore, Helen, Mary, Angelo, Louis, John, Vilonda, Mathilda, and Emma. (Courtesy St. Aloysius Parish Cookbook, 1928—2003)

Giacomini

Constantino & Caterina. Both came from Purello, Italy. He was a coal miner and she was a homemaker. They had 6 children: Domenic, Helen, Linda, Selina, Lena and Merino, in the center. (Courtesy St. Aloysius Parish Cookbook, 1928—2003)

Golabs

Felix & Maria Golab. He was from Krzywaczka, Poland and she was born in Palcza, Poland. They were married in Poland on March 17, 1907. He was a coal miner at Coal Mine A, in Devereux. They had 6 children: John & Edward (born in Poland), Mary, Josephine, Sophia and Elizabeth. (Courtesy St. Aloysius Parish Cookbook, 1928—2003)

Paoni

John and Albina (Biscontini). Both came from Perugia, Italy around 1889. He was a coal miner and she was a homemaker. They had 11 children: 2 died of the 1918 flu, Ross, Josephine, Sesto, Katherine, Susan, Joseph, John, Fred, and Jennie. (Courtesy St. Aloysius Parish Cook Book, 1928—2003)

Rodolfi

Joseph & Clara. They came from Gubbio, Italy. He was a coal miner and she was a homemaker. They raised her nieces and nephews: Geno, Mary, & Freida Damiani. They also had five other children: Joe Freddie, Olga, Rita, Jessie, and Eleanor (Rudy). (Courtesy Rudy Rodolfi)

Simko

Steve A. & Mary E. They were Slovak-Austrian-Hungarian
Europeans. He was a coal miner and self-employed farmer. She
was a homemaker. They had 12 children: Mary, Sister Anne
(above), Kathryn, Stephen, Andrew, John, Emory, Frank,
Louis, Tom, Regina, and James. (courtesy St. Aloysius Parish
Cook Book, 1928—2003)

Random Pictures and Scenes

about Devereux Heights

Plate 1. A house full of Paonis on Mayden Ave. I can almost see Father Al preaching to the multitudes in the front yard, with Mr. Fofi waving his fist from his yard. (Courtesy of Nancy Bartlett)

Plate 2. Postcard drawing of the dining room of the Mayden Country House. It was an addition to the north side of their home. (Courtesy SVC)

Eddy Coal Co. Presents Vacation Checks To Miners

Paul Salveson, extreme right, secretary-treasurer of the Eddy Coal Co. mine at Cantrall, passes out vacation pay checks to miners before they enter the mine to work the last 4 p. m. to midnight shift, before starting their two week vacation yesterday. Left to right are William Usapict, Springfield, financial secretary local 7746, United Mine Workers of America; Tony Antonacci, Riverton; Sam Williamson, Sherman; Ernie Willis, Springfield; Harold Wolf, Springfield; Frank Antonacci, Riverton, and Salveson. They received $140 vacation pay if they worked continuously during the preceeding 12 months, an increase of $40 over the same period last year. Bryan Eddy, president of the company, stated that 90 per cent of the coal produced was consumed in the Springfield area. It is the only mine operating during the summer months in Sangamon county, and since last year's vacation was worked 178 days. An innovation this year will be an employes picnic to be held at Lake Springfield during the vacation period which ends July 9, according to an announcement made to employes yesterday by William E. Dart, office manager.

Plate 3. Miners worked at the Eddy Mine in Cantrall when the Devereux Mine closed. The miner on the left had not washed yet. Around 1940 (Courtesy Jim & Nancy Bartlett)

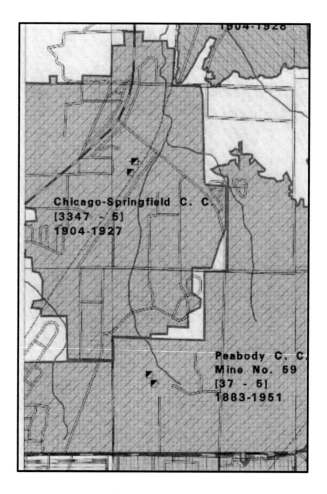

Plate 4. The 2 square boxes (top ones) mark the shafts of the Devereux Mine, No. 3347. The other mine at the bottom is the one most folks in Devereux remember and get confused with with the Devereux Mine. (Courtesy SVC)

Plate 5. c. 1912 Sand Hill Class. Second Row left side is
Josephine Golab; the next two girls are the Galassi sisters. The
Top Row, sixth over from the left is Bob Bartlett, Sr. (Courtesy
Jim & Nancy Bartlett)

Plate 6. Piper School 1940. This is Mrs. Mueller's classes, grades 1 through 4, from right to left. Dominic Giacomini, a first grader, is the 2nd student in the first row on the right. In the other classroom are grades 5 – 8 presided over by Mrs. Ava Thomas Weber. (Courtesy Dominic Giacomini)

Plate 7. Piper School Classes 5-8. Left Row: Betty Beja, Albert Schobier, Joe Beja, Doris Piper and ? Moffitt. Middle Row: ? Girl, Ray Bennett, Jim Moffit, John Proctor, Leonard Diaz, and Rita Banning. Right Row: Barb Galassi, Neil Criemwoody, Mary Bartlet, and Jim Bartlett. Teacher is Ava Thomas Weber. 1942. (Courtesy Jim & Nancy Bartlett)

Plate 8. Bob "Yogi" Yoggerst standing on the old railroad bed in his Lineal Park, near his house. The creek at the bottom of the ravine is at the lower left in the picture.

Plate 9. This is a trestle similar to the one for the C&A freight track about an eighth of a mile to the Devereux Mine, traversing the ravine at the cross-over (when the tracks were on the east side).

Plate 10. The Simko Family Farm was situated on 114 acres just south and east of the original Devereux Heights plat. The family house faced Mayden Ave. The Simkos sold the land to Gail Wanless who developed it into Twin Lakes subdivision in the mid-'60s.The Simkos had 8 sons and 4 daughters. During WWII, 7 sons were in the service. The Simko Farm was the only working farm around Devereux. This picture shows Steve, Frank, John, Andy, Louis, Tommy, Joe and Jim. Taken Aug. 1966, right before they sold the farm for development (Courtesy Jim & Nancy Bartlett.)

Plate 11. The Roll Inn Tavern & Dance Hall on North Dirksen Parkway. No changes when they sold it except the name. It was built by the Golabs and began operation in 1941. It was on 3.25 acres, bordering the north end of the village of Devereux Heights, just east of where the Chicago-Springfield Coal Mine once stood. It was known for playing polka music for over 35 years. (Courtesy of Mary Yoggerst)

Plate 12. The Roll Inn, a popular dance hall and tavern, had a very large dance floor with a capacity of 300. Betty (Golab) Zrillic and Josephine (Golab) Paciorek are having fun dancing in the middle. (Courtesy of Mary Yoggerst)

Plate 13. This kind of Springfield trolley car is similar to
the ones that served Devereux from the Interurban track
on the west side of the village. Around 1930.(Courtesy SVC)

Plate 14. Gene Giacomini died in a mining
accident at the Peabody #59 Mine.

Plate 15. Wooden bridge similar to the North Street (later, Randy Street) one over the ravine and train tracks, as Rudy Rodolfi remembers, "with no guard rails." She recalled the 75-ft. span as a little girl "and then, all of a sudden, it was gone."

Plate 16. The long-time bench in front of the Jail-house Tavern is being used by then bartender Ernie "Killer" Danner during a break. The blocks it sits on are from the remnants of the foundation from the Zinc Works. Jim Bartlett said, "Everybody from around here used those big blocks for foundations for houses and buildings." (Courtesy Jim & Nancy Bartlett)

THE SALVATION ARMY
GIRLS SOFTBALL TEAM
SPRINGFIELD ILL

Plate 17. This picture was taken when Rudy Rodolfi was a senior at Lanphier High School, so 1945. This was not a Devereux team although several of the girls were from the village. This was close to the beginning of her 18-year career in softball which culminated in her induction into the Springfield IL Sports Hall of Fame. 1st row(L to R): Dorothy Paoni, Tony Galassi, Tillie Galassi, Jean Staples, and Dorothy Gentry. 2nd Row: Betty Gill, Louise Beja, Betty Nelson, Pinky Princiballic, Liz Gillock, and Rudy Rodolfi. 3rd Row: Fred Paoni (mgr), Helen Quinnegan, Major Fred Brewer (sponsor), Kathleen Paoni, and John Cavitt (preacher). (Courtesy Rudy Rodolfi)

News came this week that Springfield will have a new baseball team to watch next summer. We truly hope the Springfield Sliders — nice turtle logo, by the way — are a big success. Springfield has certainly had its ups and downs with baseball leagues — yet, baseball and softball have always been popular as a participation sport in the capital city. Today's photo goes back 61 years to the 1946 Madison Furniture Co. girls softball team. Charles Madison, then the owner of Madison Furniture, 11th and South Grand Avenue, was the team's sponsor, and its manager was George Casey, who also happened to be a sports writer for the newspaper. Bottom row (left to right): Melba Conlee, Georgia Hardisty, Jane Vasconcellos and bat boy Bobby Degner. Center row: Marceline Steskal, Florence Capranica, Theresa Joyce, Corrine Jallas and Alice Folder. Top row: George Casey, Eleanor Rudolph, Mary Moak, Amelia Leonard and Charles Madison.

If you have an old photograph — you decide what constitutes old — that you think others would enjoy seeing in the newspaper, please call editorial page editor Mike Matulis at 788-1508.

Plate 18. Rudy Rodolfi also played with Madison Furniture and so did some of her Devereux friends. (Courtesy SJ-R, 12-1-07)

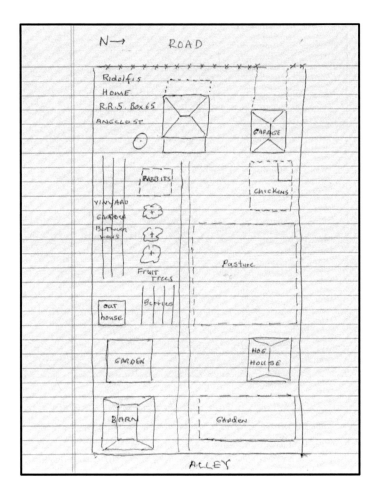

Plate 19. Rodolfi's back lot on Angelo Street during the Depression (c. 1935). The lot was 102 ft wide by 250 ft deep or around 0.6 acre. (Rudy Rodolfi)

269

Plate 20. Chicago-Springfield Mine Layout. 1- tipple, 2-air or escape shaft, 3- hoist shaft, 4-engine room, 5-wash house, 6-office, 7- scales, and 8- blacksmith shop. The ladder-lines are underground tunnels. The railroad is marked "Alton RR," east of the structures. (Courtesy ISGS)

Do you remember?

Students at Pryor School are shown in this photo taken in 1927. The school, located on Vincent Street in Devereaux Heights, was later renamed Piper, which closed its doors for good this spring. Only Virginia Kinzora is deceased of the eight students who graduated from Pryor School on June 7, 1927. Those seven listed on the graduation program are Fred Bidolli, Emma Fix, Erman Fofi, Helen Lenn, Elizabeth Marconi, Irene Menendez and Fred Paoni. Pictured are, first row from left, Tom Penington, Eddie Buchnick, John Paoni, Joe Washlick, Woodrow Robinson, Edward Aldrich, Mat Richno, Dolcedo Micheletti, Fred Paoni and Frank Mullman; second row from left,

Dock Paoni, Mary Galassi, Helen Galassi, Mary Galassi, Ann Simko, Irene Menendez, Jessie Paoni, Helen Rondelli, Linda Giacomini, Emma Fix and Catherine Simko; third row from left, Bubbles Tomashavich, Fanny Kratachvil, unknown, Clara Galassi, Vincent Galassi, Angelo Galassi, Dominic Giacomini, John Bedolli, Stanley Murnick and Mary Simko; last row from left Jessie Penington, Joe Borowick, Mike Fix, Tillie Micheletti, Elizabeth Paoni, Ada Galassi and Mrs. Cressy. (Persons who wish may submit photos for this State Journal-Register feature by contacting Do You Remember Editor at the newspaper, 6th St.)

Plate 21. This is the only picture I could find of a Pryor School class. It is a combined picture of the grade school classes at the end of the 1926-1927 school year. (Courtesy the SJ-R)

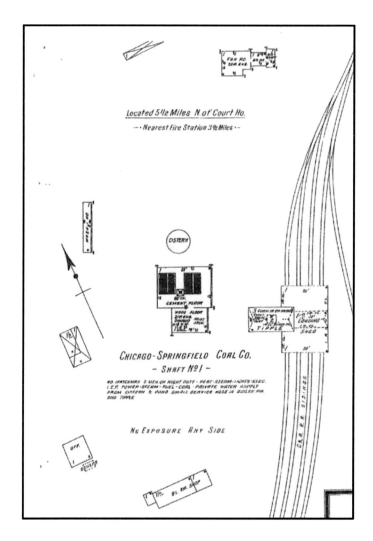

Plate 22. Devereux Mine tipple & associated structures. (Courtesy Illinois State Geological Survey)

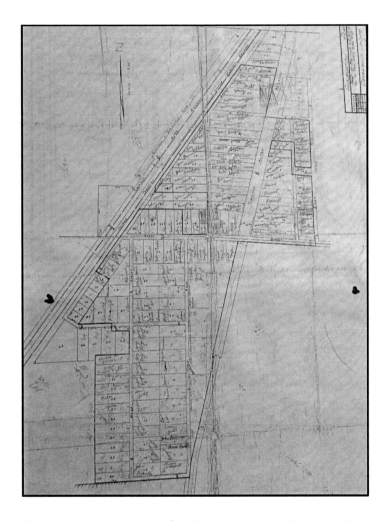

Plate 23. This plat drawn for the Annexation Plan in 1963 shows the "two Devereuxs." The original plat at the top is what I call North Devereux Heights, with Mayden Avenue as the demarcation line. South Devereux is everything below that line and is actually the Piper Addition. The road that goes north and south is Piper Road. At the bottom is Sangamon Avenue, going east and west, and is cut out of the picture but is almost the bottom line of the picture.

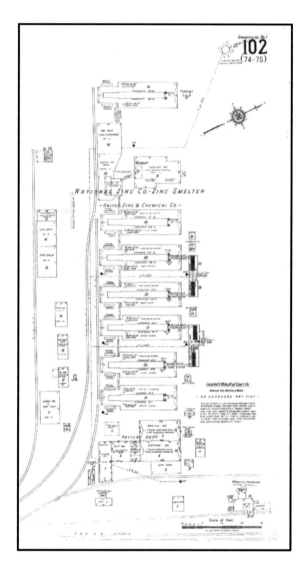

Plate 24. The Zinc Works included 12 furnaces, ore sheds, mixing sheds, engine house, water tower, blacksmith shop, machine shop, potter dept. with drying chambers, & magnetic separator. Notice several RR lines called sidings. Approx. 20 acres in the drawing. (Courtesy ISGS)

274

Plate 25. Rendering of the completed Zinc Works complex, from the Devereux Hts. Plat Sales poster. Accompanying it were drawings of attractive company housing additions. 1913.

Plate 26. The "crossover point" in this picture is where the creek goes from north to east and then straightens out again. The tracks follow it, going from the west side of the ravine to the east side, which necessitated the building of the trestle. Bob Yoggerst heard from his mother-in-law, Mary Golab, that townspeople would use that jog in the creek as a pass for their cattle crossing under the trestle back in the twenties.

Plate 27. This 100-year-old bench reminds me of the benches the village women would sit on in front of their houses to talk. It is in Mary & Bob Yoggersts' side yard. It belonged to her grand-parents, Jacob & Katie Soltys, who lived in south Springfield.

Plate 28. This is the present, renovated residence that used to be the Mayden White House or Country House on the south side of Mayden Avenue. Notice the rectangular addition in the front or north side of the house. That was the restaurant.

Plate 29. Coal Loading Dock off of S. Interurban Ave.
(From the 1913 Plat Sales Poster.)

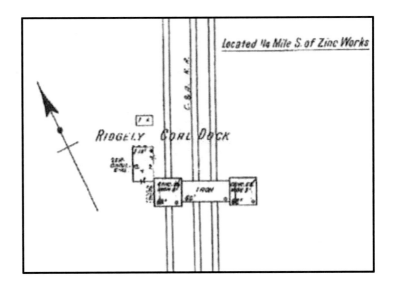

Plate 29b. The Ridgely Coal Dock. This structure is the
same one in the above diagram. (Courtesy ISGS)

Plate 30. Dr. Dominic Sterbini, M.D. Educated in Italy, he served in the Italian army in WWI. He practiced medicine in Springfield for 15 years before moving to Colfax, Illinois, near Bloomington. (His obituary)

Plate 31. The Rodolfi House on Angelo Street. These "four-room houses" were sold to miners, who worked at the Devereux Mine, by the company. Many of the original houses looked just like this one, porch and all. Around 1920. Notice the twin doors. (Courtesy Rudy Rodolfi)

Plate 32. Loveable "Crax" was Joe Freddie "Fredo" Rodolfi.
As helpful to all around him as he was flawed.
(Courtesy Judy Hawks)

Plate 33. The "Devereux Sisters," I'll call them, because this second generation of village women were an inseparable team. They attended St. Al's Church together and were fast friends all of their lives. I wish I had interviewed them together; what a story they could have told me. Lf. To Rt.: Lena (Giacomini) Ostenberg, Olga (Rodolfi) Handley, Sofia (Golab) Geyston, and Florence (Kunz) Galassi. Only Florence is still with us today. (Courtesy Judy Hawks)

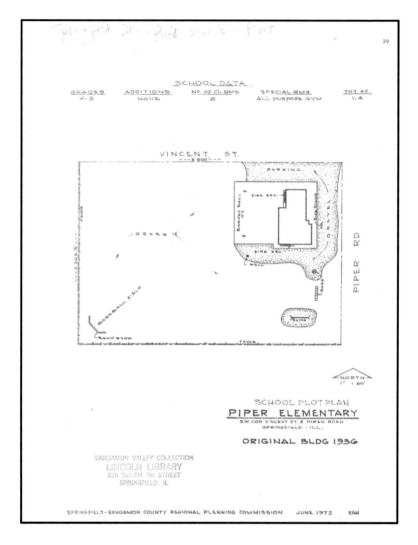

Plate 34. Piper School Lot (1936). The previous schoolhouse was west of the new school and was torn down after Piper was built. (Courtesy SVC)

Plate 35. The sewer pumping station on Mayden Avenue. This is another defining Devereux Heights icon of sorts. It was put in as a result of the annexation to Springfield. The 36 -nch main broke a couple years ago and the city had to dig 24 feet down to locate and repair it. Notice the chain-link fence: it guards the sewer easement running just inside the fence leading to the old railway.

Plate 36. Holliday's Pond on Angelo Street. On top of the hill in the background you can usually see two alpacas and a llama grazing below the old railbed. They make you look twice. Donna's son Johnnie fishes from the shaded gazebo on the right edge of the pond.

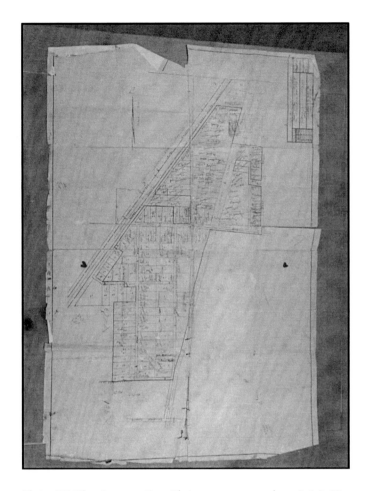

Plate 37. The Annexation Plat was prepared on 8-14-65 by consulting engineering firm Lawrence C. Auby, Jr. The 24" x 36" tattered map was used by Helen Sefick who filled in each lot owner's name in Devereux. The plat excluded only 19 lots which elected to stay out of the city. (Courtesy of Gladys Sefick)

Plate 38. Vineyard in the backyard of Assunta Galassi's family
house on Donna Street. Devereux had grapes growing on
probably every lot in the village at one time. On the right is a
grape arbor; they could be elaborate as you will see in another
picture below. Helen Galassi is the young girl. (Courtesy of Gladys
Sefick)

Plate 39. Fall mushrooming. These three ladies are preparing what villagers called "carina" mushrooms. U of I mycologist Dr. Andrew Miller identified them as *Grifola frondosa,* commonly called hen of the woods, also called sheep or rams head. They are usually found at the base of oak trees. (Courtesy of Al Kenal)

Plate 40. Let's party! This kind of impromptu gathering in the back yard of one of Devereux's families was a common occurrence. All they had to say was, "Hey, let's get together Friday night," and a dozen or so neighbors made it happen. Notice the keg as the centerpiece. The time period may have been in the 1940s. (Courtesy of Al Kenal)

Plate 41. Village women would meet around the "big tree at the Simko Farm," just south of Mayden Avenue, where Twin Lakes is now. This was in 1966, although it could have been back in the '30s, when it was probably started. I wish I knew the tradition. (Courtesy of Al Kenal)

Plate 42. Helen "H" (Galassi) Sefick. Kind, tough, and determined, this lady helped collect flowers and money for families who lost loved ones. She also was a major force in bringing Devereux Heights into the city of Springfield. "This was her pose when she laughed," commented daughter-in-law Gladys. (Courtesy of Gladys Sefick)

Plate 43. Camp 4 food preparation by George Kenal's wife, Mary. It looked like quite a few of the family members would be eating. This camp area was located about three miles upstream from the village of Devereux, toward Riverton. (Courtesy Al Kenal)

Plate 44. George Kenal's long and elaborate grape arbor in his back yard on Angelo St., with an unidentified boy. This shows the lengths villagers would go through to grow grapes for their wines. (Courtesy Al Kenal)

Plate 45. Vince Galassi with his daughter Laura in front of his garage on Peoria Road. He was the "mover and shaker" in pushing the annexation plan. With Vince's resourcefulness and street savvy, a writer covering the North-End beat might have dubbed him "Mr. Devereux Heights." Opponents of the plan may have had other names for him. (c. 1961)

Plate 46. This is a boarding house for single miners near a coal mine. This is probably very similar to the 27-room one that the Devereux Mine company built for its miners at the same time it built the other mine structures.

Plate 47. Devereux Height's Sewing Club. These 20 women met for many years. Some younger women in the village called it the Gossip Club. It included prominent women like Helen Sefick, Eva Antonacci, Emma Bedolli, Tootsie Galassi and Mary Mitchell. (1951) (Courtesy of Gladys Sefick)

Plate 48. Mess of fish to be fried and sold at the Jailhouse Tavern. These intrepid fisherman braved the cold to ice-fish the Sangamon River. Lt. to Rt. are George Kenal, Sesto "Brains" Paoni, "Casey" Dallamorte, and Al's Uncle Joe Galassi. Early '60s. (Courtesy Al Kenal)

Plate 49. The always smiling Pam Meyers-Jerome, longest owner of the iconic Jailhouse Tavern in Devereux. Notice how the back bar shows itself as both elegant and inviting. If walls could talk!

Plate 50. The Knights of Columbus Building at the southwest corner of Devereux Heights. It has around five acres in all, which includes a park shelter with shade trees around it, to the east.

Plate 51. The Barn Tavern on West Street. The tavern was in operation from the 1940s to around 1964. This was the front of the tavern or the back—they both looked the same, I was told. This was taken in 1978 as it was being torn down to make room for houses. (Courtesy of Lou Menendez)

Plate 52. This mine, just southeast of Devereux Heights, had several names because of several owners. Springfield No. 1 (1899-1904), Jones & Adams (1905-1908), Peerless (1908-1929), and Peabody No. 59 (1930-1951). Even "New Jones." (Courtesy SVC)

Plate 53. Here I am showing Mark McDonald the original plat for the village of Devereux Heights. We are taping his PBS program "Illinois Stories" that will feature the village in September's segment. (Courtesy of Michael Jerome)

Plate 54. Four of my research assistants. These folks were among those who provided stories and facts about the village. Lt. to Rt. Brad Mills, Bob & Mary Yoggerst, and Nancy Bartlett. This was At Pam's Jailhouse Tavern during the taping of "Illinois Stories." (Courtesy of Michael Jerome, Pam's son)

Plate 55. Mark McDonald, "Illinois Stories" producer and host, interviewing Al Kenal, lifetime resident of the Village. Few things escaped Al's attention in 81 years. (Courtesy of Michael Jerome)

Plate 56. Charlie Bedolli, a life-long resident of the village, drives home a point to Mark McDonald. He is explaining wine making as well as bootlegging as integral parts of Devereux. (Courtesy Michael Jerome)

Plate 57. Springfield Mobsters. On right is Sam Zito, one of two brothers of Springfield's godfather, Frank Zito. Sam was in charge of the liquor trade in the '20s and is here visiting a Devereux client. I'll use "alleged" in front of mobsters, godfather, etc. (Courtesy of Candice Cummins)

Plate 58. Susie Paoni posing with a mobster in front of his Car in Devereux in the 1920s. (Courtesy Candice Cummins)

Plate 59. The only picture approaching a Devereux Heights landscape I could find. 1920s. The caption reads "Speck's Dog". "Speck" is Ross Paoni. (Courtesy of Candice Cummins)

NOTE: Candice Cummins, who donated the above three pictures, states that they are from a collection of "Paoni Family History by Jennie T. Paoni-Willis (my grandmother). We sat together in Mountain View, Arkansas, going over these pictures."

Miscellaneous

Ownership Origins of the Devereux Property

It wasn't easy tracing the property rights of the land occupied by the Devereux Mine and Devereux Heights. The "this-half-of-that-quarter-of-that-part" stuff is hard to follow. With the help of our capable local historian Curtis Mann, I waded through the legalese and came up with the following.

The land Devereux Mine and its settlement eventually rested on was located on two adjoining parcels whose legal descriptions are: Parcel 1: E ½ of SE ¼ of Section 11 and Parcel 2: W ½ of SW ¼ of Section 12. Each parcel contained 80 acres or a total of 160 acres.

The land patent passing ownership from the United States Government to the first private owner of Parcel 1 was granted on June 10, 1835 to David Spear and his wife Ann Marie. The land patent for Parcel 2 was granted to Ninian W. Edwards on October 29, 1835.

The Spears sold their 80 acres to Ninian W. Edwards in August 1835, who now owned the entire 160 acres. Ninian then sold the 160 acres to his mother, Elvira L. Edwards, on November 11, 1835.

Next in the testamentary will there followed a curious statement. "The negro slave Savary is to be taken into this division [with] $600 (his valuation) deducted from son Ninian." (The Northwest Ordinance banned slavery in the new states comprising it, and Illinois was one such state. To reinforce the prohibition the Illinois Constitution of 1848 specially forbade slavery. My guess is that Savary was transferred under involuntary servitude to Ninian.)

Elvira L. Edwards, willed it to her children when she passed.

The Edwards' four children—Ninian W., A.G., Benjamin S. and Margret Edwards Lane—sold the land on August 13, 1839, to two men, Norris J. and Paul J. Hoffman, who lived in Philadelphia, PA. Possibly brothers, they were according to the 1860 Census an accountant and a farmer.

The Hoffmans held onto the two tracts until June 3, 1859, when they sold them together to Caleb Birchall.

Caleb Birchall willed the 160 acres to his daughter Cordelia S. M., who married Phil Warren.

The Warrens owned the tract and eventually sold it to the Devereux group which began the Chicago-Springfield Coal Co. The Warrens also granted the all-important coal rights to the mine on October 20, 1902, and a few months later sold a right-of-way over 3.73 acres of the land to the mine.

On February 26, 1907, the Warrens sold 30.3 more acres (plus another 0.05 acre parcel) to "George Wood et al," where Wood acted as grantee for the mine company— the "et al" being the other owners jointly. That conveyance and three other small land transfers within the next two years were all to United Zinc, just west of the mine.

The final conveyance chain I followed was on August 19, 1909, when the coal company gave another right-of-way for a road near the mine.

The local newspaper covered the story that Devereux and his group purchased "over 100 acres for the mine and the subsequent Devereux Heights Addition," which was in fact 160 acres—the two tracts that began with the two land patents.

Coal Miner Hooliganism

The oldest source I found of miners at the new Devereux Mine was a newspaper story in *the Illinois State Register* on October 17, 1910. The mine would have been running for six years.

The incident was headlined as "Badly Injured At Devereux 'Patch." A Slavic miner by the name of John Backaanch who lived in Devereux was savagely attacked by a Lithuanian miner by the name of "Joe" early on Sunday morning [the day before the article appeared.]

The victim told the reporter, whose beat happened to be St. John's Hospital, he had been injured on the hand at the mine on Saturday and the doctor patched him up and placed his arm in a sling for a few days.

Sunday morning he could not sleep because of the throbbing pain, so he got up and left the boarding house for a walk around the patch.

"He had walked but a short distance when he passed a house that a number of Lithunian [sic] miners were congregated, and who, it is said, had been drinking since the evening before. [A] miner . . . came out and into the street and struck him over the head with a board." Backaanch was defenseless with his arm unusable. The man continued to assail him with a knife. The report explained [he] was . . . stabbed a number of times about the face, forehead and shoulder. One cut on the nose was so deep that it almost cut the nose in two, and in length reached almost to one of his eyes."

I wondered if the police got involved. There seems to be more to the story than meets the eye, but we can only speculate. The victim said he could think of no reason for the sudden attack and that "he had known the man by sight for about three years and had never had any trouble with him."

This incident might give us some insight into the horrendous working conditions below in the mine and how they could have contributed to animosities among the various ethnic groups, most of whom could not speak the other's language.

The Lawless Twenties

The following NEWSPAPER articles will give you a shocking look inside the village of Devereux during the Prohibition days of the "Roaring Twenties." It is in stark contrast to the community I laid out in most of this book. Some might think it would be best if this aspect of the village were lost to history. I bring it to light for you because every town has two sides, and this is Devereux's underbelly, at least during the '20s. Each story is restated by me from the *Illinois State Journal* newspaper, which Curtis Mann dug up at my request.

●

Just recently, in the *Springfield Journal-Register* (June 3, 2019), there appeared a feature by the Sangamon County Historical Society about a certain Servia Diaz and his involvement in racketeering and booze in our capital city just months before the despised law went into effect. It began, "The 14 gallons of whiskey federal agents seized on

May 30, 1919, made Servia Diaz Springfield's first officially recognized Prohibition bootlegger."

The thing that caught my eye as I skimmed the lines was that "Diaz made the whiskey in the basement of his home in Devereux Heights, then outside the northeast city limits." The cops took the breach seriously and Diaz's new address after his conviction was Leavenworth Federal Prison for two years of a four-year sentence. In addition, he had to cough up $600 in fines and periodic meetings with his parole officer in Decatur, IL.

It so happens that Servia Diaz had a brother, Frank. The latter was Lou Menendez's great-uncle (i.e., his grandmother's brother). His "Uncle Frank" was running his own bootlegging operation out of part of the basement in the old Menendez house across from the Barn Tavern—the one with the distinctive gambrel roof still on West Street—and was clever enough not to have gotten caught. Rumor had it that Frank was a partner with the legendary mobster Frank Zito who resided in Springfield.

•

August 30, 1924. DEPUTY SHERIFFS AND U.S. AGENTS UNITE FOR RAIDS: NAB ELEVEN; SEIZE RUM There was a series of raids by local sheriffs and U.S. Prohibition Enforcement Agents in Devereux Heights and Shale Bluffs, a small village southeast of Springfield. Those "resulted in the arrest of eleven men and the confiscation of beer, wine, and mule valued at thousands of dollars."

In Devereux Heights they raided five resorts [houses serving alcohol and more] known as "can joints" from the fact that most of the stuff sold was home brew beer delivered in tin cans.

The agents destroyed hundreds of gallons of the illegal alcohol and arrested the bartenders and the proprietors. They were Frank Strode, Joe Csiha, Pete Vittoni, Joe Botwenis, Pasqual Fofi, and Ralph Cardoni.

•

May 27, 1926. DEVEREUX HEIGHTS QUIET WHILE HOMEBREW RESORTS FEAR ACTION OF RAIDERS "Devereux Heights, where open house, night and day, has been quite the fad in these Volsteadian days, entertained no visitors yesterday." The reason there was there no activity in "the

319

colony's well-known homebrew," was because all the alcohol "had been dumped in anticipation of visits of dry raiders." This was precipitated "within an hour after the shooting of Thomas Langford, a federal agent at 15th and Taft Streets [in Springfield]." "The word spread quickly through the Heights—and the folks out there knew what to do and did it."

•

October 16, 1926. GUN FIRED AS PAIR BATTLE; TWO WITNESSES BEING SOUGHT. "Leo Dellamorte, 35, miner residing in Devereux Heights, was shot and instantly killed at 1:45 o'clock this Saturday morning." Witnesses said that Dellamorte was trying to rob two customers as they left a drink resort operated by Carlo Pountellcci. The owner saw the incident and struggled with Dellamorte for the gun, which went off, killing the assailant.

•

October 24, 1926. DEVEREUX HEIGHTS AGAIN The Sangamon County grand jury has been asked to consider another killing in Devereux Heights . . . where lawlessness and disorder are entirely too frequent." It goes on to castigate the village for its violence and notorious behavior. The article ends by saying "it is the duty of the county to clean up such spots. . . ."

Flawed: Mayor Devereux

As was alluded to in the first chapter, Mayor Devereux's administration was universally assailed as a machine politician by both parties, both newspapers—the morning Republican *Journal* and the evening Democratic *Register*—and the public at large. So, to give you a better understanding of the political man and his reputation, the following are excerpts from newspaper articles that bare on the man. He was elected twice, 1902—1904 and 1904—1906. These journalists give you a look, mainly back, over those years in office and why they didn't want him staying in office.

September 30, 1906 [ILLINOIS STATE] REGISTER ARRAIGNS DEVEREUX, *Illinois State Journal*. The Republican paper reports "a scathing attack" on the mayor by his party's own newspaper, the *State Register*. The article headline was "Our Shame!" as the Register accused itself of poor judgement in endorsing Devereux a second time when it knew from his first term how his administration aided "the open carnival of vice and crime that . . . flaunt their shame in boastful exultation." The two-column article goes on and on decrying "the damnable vices that are under the protection and tolerance of those sworn to suppress them."

●

March 31, 1907 ELECTION OF A MAYOR, *Illinois State Register.* "The issues involved necessarily brought up an eruption of bitterness and intense political feeling" because of the previous Devereux administration "Mayor Devereux's record of unfaithfulness to his party, his city and his official trust, made it imperative that the State Register and every genuine democrat oppose his renomination and re-election." It goes on to say that some Democrat machine loyalists decided to put Devereux up to run a third term. The paper pointed out that "ten years of machine domination, ring-rule and maladministration" were enough for the public to stomach. A group of patriotic citizens prevailed in convincing both sides to vote for "an independent candidate . . . with a clean record." And so Devereux' reign was over.

●

April 4, 1907, HOW IT HAPPENED, *Illinois State Register*. "The acrimony and asperity of the defeated Devereux machine . . . dragged the ticket down to defeat . . . The voters were anxious to defeat Devereux." The paper emphasized that he lost in a landslide, in 21 out of 32 precincts: "The defeat could not have been more overwhelming." The "gang," those machine pols who backed Devereux, blamed the loss on The Register: "The gang flatters the State Register by giving this paper the entire credit for Devereux's defeat." It goes on to flatter itself when it proclaimed that "[We] stood for principle and for the party, and that it fought "boss" rule, and government by gangster."

Message in a Piece of Coal

Let us end with a happy story. Within three years of the "C-S Mine" opening, a "curiosity" was found at the bottom of the new mine. It excited the local paper (slow news day?) and appeared on page 8 of the November 30, 1906 *Illinois State Register*.

Miners discovered a piece of coal that had a small inscription and date carved in it. "The entire inscription cannot be distinguished on account of the faintness of some of the letters. [But] several of the letters were very plain . . ," and it was obvious to all that it was a part of a sonnet band, no doubt written by a miner in love. The miners who extracted the foot-square piece of coal said it had originally been part of a longer piece about six feet in length that was no longer to be found.

The piece had come out of a pit car and loaded onto a flat car ready for shipment when it was found. "[It] is a piece of bottom coal, and was taken from the main east entry, at a place 240 feet below the surface of the earth."

It was taken to Mayor Devereux's office and later was placed in the State Museum by mine superintendent George Streible.

About the Author

Ken Mitchell is a local author who has written 16 books and several shorter pieces. He has degrees from Millikin University in history and political science and University of Illinois—Springfield in biology and education.

He has had an enjoyable and varied 40-year career, starting and running several businesses, including real estate, farming, horse breeding and insurance. He was a commodities broker, corporate recruiter and trainer. He ended his business career in sales and marketing. His career is documented in his autobiography, *My Working Life: Finding Meaning through Twists & Turns* (2016).

Among his interests are flying (he's a licensed pilot), sports cars, world religions, reading, and tennis. . . oh, and writing.

Ken has five living children—Robb, an Army Colonel; his twin brother Todd, also an Army Colonel; Brett, an Uber driver; Ladd, in IT; and Zemfira, a recent college graduate. His first daughter, Anne, died at birth and, as an angel, has been watching over him and her mother ever since.

Ken and his wife, Karen Kelly, a retired teacher at Fairview Elementary School, live in Springfield, IL, with their daughter. They have five grandchildren: Brody, Tegan, Simon, Calliope and Audree. Ken and Karen enjoy traveling, especially in and around the San Juan Mountains in southwest Colorado.

Ken is a past member of the National Speakers Association and a Certified Toastmaster. As a public speaker and trainer, Ken leads seminars on writing family histories and memoirs. He is also available for group speaking through his website, www.KenMitchellBooks.com.

 Seagull Press Publishing • Editing • Consulting • Speaking • Seminars

To Order Quickly

Call 217-787-7100

When leaving a message do not give credit card information

Or

Go to our Website at

kenmitchellbooks.com

PayPal or Major Credit Cards accepted

Seagull Press will donate a portion of the profits from this book to assist author and minister, Wayne Muller, in his charity work, Bread for the Journey.

> Its Mission: To find people with strength and vision who are passionate about improving their community, and help them make it happen.

> Its Vision: To nurture the seed of generosity that exists in every human heart.

> For a description of this work, go to breadforthejourney.org. If you're interested in starting a local chapter, contact the charity directly.

I wholeheartedly recommend Muller's best-selling book *How Then, Shall We Live?: Four Simple Questions That Reveal the Beauty and Meaning of Our Lives.* In it he poses and then answers these four profound questions in a wonderful narrative:

Who am I?
What do I love?
How shall I live, knowing I will die?
What is my gift to the family of the earth?